THE NEW BOSS

The New Boss is the result of a special collaboration between Kogan Page and Redline Wirtschaft, Germany's leading business publisher. Selected best-selling titles previously published by Redline Wirtschaft are translated into English and published by Kogan Page to ensure a worldwide distribution.

THE NEW BOSS

How to Survive the First 100 Days

Peter Fischer

KOGAN
PAGE

London and Philadelphia

Publisher's note

Every possible effort has been made to ensure that the information in this book is accurate at the time of going to press, and the publishers and authors cannot accept responsibility for any errors or omissions, however caused. No responsibility for loss or damage occasioned to any person acting, or refraining from action, as a result of the material in this publication can be accepted by the editor, the publisher or the author.

First published in Germany in 1993 by Redline Wirtschaft as *Neu auf dem Chefsessel – Erfolgreich durch die ersten 100 Tage*

First published in Great Britain and the United States in 2007 by Kogan Page Limited as *The New Boss: How to survive the first 100 days*
Reprinted 2007

Translated from German into English by David R Antal

120 Pentonville Road
London N1 9JN
United Kingdom
www.kogan-page.co.uk

525 South 4th Street, #241
Philadelphia PA 19147
USA

© 1993/2005 Redline Wirtschaft, Redline GmbH, Heidelberg, Germany, a division of Sueddeutscher Verlag I Mediengruppe
© 2007 Kogan Page

The right of Peter Fischer to be identified as the author of this work has been asserted by him in accordance with the Copyright, Designs and Patents Act 1988.

ISBN-10   0 7494 4764 8
ISBN-13   978 0 7494 4764 9

British Library Cataloguing-in-Publication Data

A CIP record for this book is available from the British Library.

Library of Congress Cataloging-in-Publication Data

Fischer, Peter.
  The new boss : how to survive the first 100 days / Peter Fischer.
       p. cm.
  ISBN-13: 978-0-7494-4764-9
  ISBN-10: 0-7494-4764-8
  1. Executives. 2. Management. 3. Organizational effectiveness. 4. Executive ability. I. Title.
  HD38.2.F57 2007
  658.4--dc22

                                                          2006102886

Typeset by Saxon Graphics Ltd, Derby
Printed and bound in Great Britain by MPG Books Ltd, Bodmin, Cornwall

Contents

Preface

Most people would agree that starting a new job is a challenge, whatever the role. A number of questions need to be addressed such as: Who are the key players within the company? Which tasks should be prioritized and which ones can be put on hold? Which decisions need to be taken immediately and which can be postponed? How can I be sure that I have correctly understood what is expected of me? Will my colleagues support me in my objectives?

Most executives will also tell you they need a 'flying start', as there is no time to contemplate what they don't know. Opportunities like this don't come along every day. Many executives have a great deal of experience of moving from position to position and are therefore comfortable with the fast pace of the business world. A closer look also reveals that there is little room for errors or experimenting. The pressure to perform is tough, as shareholders regularly scrutinize results. In many cases, the new executive will find that first impressions count, and personal reputations are always at risk.

A look at many client organizations these days reveals pressure for success on a global scale. This means that innovation, consistently high standards and speed are of the essence in the face of less transparent and tougher competition. In comparison, cultural diversity and virtual relationships seem relatively straightforward. More importantly, the need to deploy resources flexibly means few executives have longer than three years to make their contributions felt –

indeed many barely have 18 months. In addition to this, the growing complexity from organizations trying to respond to fast-changing technologies, legal frameworks and markets brings both the possibilities and the pitfalls inherent in a leadership transition into focus. Indeed the objective of this book is to reveal the 'power of change' – that is to say, the opportunities for introducing change and preparing for eventual success over the inevitable pitfalls intrinsic to any transition process.

Gone are the days when predecessors overlapped with the new candidate to ease the handover. Instead I find many new managers finishing assignments in one role at the same time as starting the new one. Whilst a sense of promise at the start and a heightened excitement during the executive honeymoon remain, the rising numbers in leadership transitions point to growing pressures on new managers to change and innovate. This sense of promise translates into a much-needed readiness to embrace change. As time is of the essence, new managers are tempted to push ahead with their agendas. After all, that was the reason for their appointment. It is easily forgotten that agendas need the support of key people and that, as a new manager, you ignore the less visible concerns, expectations and past achievements at your peril.

I have always been convinced of the opportunities inherent in the situation at the start. Developments over the past 10 years have reinforced that belief and encouraged me and my colleagues at fgi continuously to develop our conceptual understanding of the topic in line with the development of a range of tools and specialist support programmes for different situations at the start. My gratitude is due to the many loyal client organizations that gave us the opportunities for development in the first place. Without them, leadership transition would not have achieved recognition as a key process for introducing organizational change.

Asked if the English-speaking world needs yet another management book, I am convinced that the promise of executive honeymoons is here to stay – and that there is definitely more to say on the subject. With this book I hope to convey an enthusiasm for the promise inherent in leadership transitions and to share our experience of how to develop a 'personal transition strategy' to make that promise come true.

I am grateful to the many managers who have given me insight into their work and to the many colleagues whose questions and suggestions have contributed to the steady development of the concepts presented in these chapters. Throughout the book I will use 'we' to indicate the expertise and experience of my colleagues at fgi.

Dr Peter Fischer
Fischer Group International
Hamburg, February 2007

Introduction

DOS AND DON'TS OF SUCCESSFUL LEADERSHIP TRANSITIONS

It is the rule rather than the exception for successful executives to move on to new responsibilities every two to three years. It is a further rule that, as soon as a change in leadership is imminent, there are certain questions from all directions in the organization: When will the new executive be able to draw up a new strategy? Will her relationships with the staff be as close as her predecessor's? How will he deal with the expected market turbulence? Will he be able to establish the same credibility with our customers? Will she want to improve relationships with our internal clients? Will I get on with him? These speculations about the newcomer's first decisions and likely approach form the focus of people's attention. They are the reason why past experiences with and failures of the new person are discussed in company cafeterias, and no finance journal misses out on stories about current or expected changes at the top. They are also the reason why the newcomer needs to be aware of the stories circulating ahead of his start, as this forms part of a delicate yet decisive dynamic between hope for a 'better' future and uncertainty and concerns about what might be in store.

Considering that each change costs approximately two and a half times the newcomer's annual salary, it makes sense to ensure this investment pays off and to find out about the dos and don'ts of successful leadership transitions.

John Gabarro, a professor of human resource management at Harvard Business School, is one of the few academics to have studied the factors affecting the success of changes in leadership. His early research examining the process of top executives taking over their positions still holds true:

- Industry insiders were considerably more successful than *industry outsiders*. Insiders succeeded more quickly than outsiders at adapting to the new situation and distinguishing between what was important and what was not. Of course, insiders were limited by insider vision, but their ability to respond quickly made up for that potential handicap.

- The results refuted the myth of a *quick* change in leadership. In many cases, at senior levels the process of getting established in a new position extended over one to two years, as major structural and staff changes followed a change at the top. Gabarro distinguished a typical pattern of activities and observations. After three to six months, most managers had launched their first major changes. This was followed by a phase of intense observation during which the newcomer gained in-depth knowledge of the organization, which he or she applied during a second phase of change after 12–18 months.

- A crucial factor distinguishing successful from less successful leaders in new positions was the *relationship to key people*. Three out of four managers who were not successful in their new roles after 12 months had poor working relations with their key employees. They had conflicts over objectives, leadership style, and the criteria of effective performance.

These results are consistent with our experience. Executives who make the transition successfully recognize and develop key relationships. They deal adroitly with secret rivals and predecessors. They build networks in the company and are much more successful at developing mutual expectations and communicating shared objectives.

In my experience, people who successfully assume new leadership roles also have a number of other competencies that set them apart from less successful counterparts (see Figure 1). They are able to organize and communicate the many topics, issues and expectations in a clear, manageable concept. They rally employees to a vision of the road to be taken in the future and spur them on to unusual performance.

When it comes to changes in leadership, another characteristic that differentiates successful from less successful executives is their stamina, particularly in a crisis. People who succeed in a transition immediately convey confidence that the chosen objectives will be achieved. They understand the importance of exhibiting self-confidence and are not dissuaded by obstacles that keep arising. These people have usually already changed jobs several times, so they have acquired broad knowledge about the course the process takes.

Knowing the territory, shaping the key relationships, developing a communicable vision, and imparting confidence and credibility are a few of the factors that differentiate people who take over a position successfully from those who are less successful at it. These characteristics are not innate; they are competencies acquired through practical experience. People who are successful in making transitions work seem to have developed a special kind of know-how. It therefore makes good sense to pay attention to the newcomer's experience with similar situations, especially when a tricky transition is anticipated.

We have prepared many executives for new positions over more than 10 years. Based on this experience and available research on the topic we identified seven building blocks that are common to most successful leadership transitions. In Part I, the building blocks will help you find the answers to many questions and issues that are typically faced by managers at the start of a new assignment: Who should I talk to? What are the important questions to ask? How do I manage the relationship with a disappointed contender for my role? How will I be able to tell which should be my priorities? When do I start to change things? How do I make sure I have the support I need to deliver on my promises and plans?

Part II presents practical examples of typical situations in leadership transition. How is a move from the company's own ranks different to being an external hire? What is involved in stepping into

Executives who make transitions successfully	Executives who are less successful in transitions
• Possess superior knowledge and familiarity with the field and readily distinguish between what is important and what is not	• Often come from outside the field and take too long to get their bearings
• Recognize and develop key relationships, deal adroitly with hidden rivals and predecessors, build networks in the organization, and show that they are team-oriented	• Focus too much on the tasks to be accomplished, neglect the development of working relations built on trust, and tend to prefer to work things out alone
• Know how to group the many issues and problems into a vision and to motivate the employees	• Pursue too many approaches at the same time without a persuasive strategy and focus on eliminating weak points
• Communicate with senior management on strategy and style of leadership	• Accept unclear expectations from senior management
• Have knowledge about the process of changing leadership and impart confidence and trust because they can assess developments	• Are too easily surprised, concentrate only on changes and thereby neglect the employees' need for stability and security

Figure 1 What distinguishes executives who make transitions successfully from those who are less successful

the shoes of a great predecessor? And how do I turn around a weak team?

This book concludes with case studies of situations involving international transitions. They illustrate the discussions, issues and surprises that a manager must handle in order to assume a position abroad successfully.

Part I

The seven building blocks of successful leadership transition

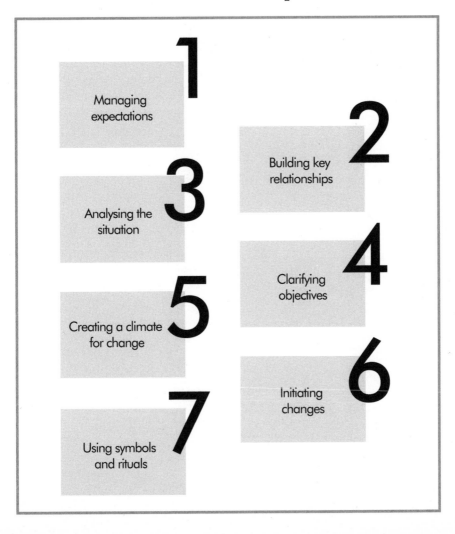

1 Managing expectations

2 Building key relationships

3 Analysing the situation

4 Clarifying objectives

5 Creating a climate for change

6 Initiating changes

7 Using symbols and rituals

Building Block 1

Managing expectations proactively

Have
a go at it

I have **full**

confidence
in you

'HAVE A GO AT IT – I HAVE FULL CONFIDENCE IN YOU!'

This sentence ended the first discussion between a regional manager and his new branch manager. The regional manager had known the newcomer for two years and considered him superbly suited to tackling the indisputably difficult job of restructuring a large branch network. Basically, taking on this position involved assuming responsibility for more than a hundred employees, implementing a new strategy and closing some of the branches.

One year later, the regional manager recommended that the branch manager should 'look around for another assignment'. It eventually emerged that the initial wholesale declaration of trust had obscured a kaleidoscope of expectations to which the two men had not agreed. 'I thought that you were focusing first on the cost side of your job' and 'I thought that you were bolstering my position in management by scoring quick successes' were just a couple of the tacit expectations. They became clear only late in the transition process, after both managers had largely staked out their own mutually divergent stances. Difficult circumstances along with a few direct conflicts then led to the unexpected termination of the assignment.

Many of these problems could have been avoided if expectations had been clarified from the beginning. Expectations are the surest thing about a change in leadership, which have an almost magical attraction and seem to bring every wish and hope for change to the surface. 'Let's see if he [she] manages to turn us round.' 'The first thing we need is more staff.' 'It would be nice to become a team at last.' All these statements are frequently heard as a change in leadership approaches. Sometimes they coalesce into expectations that are almost impossible to meet, as was the case confronting the new head of a national rail organization in Europe. He accepted an invitation from the head of state, who expected him not only to restructure the organization's portfolio, turn around unprofitable activities and resolve the perennial conflict over the financing of the railway network, but also to find his way through difficult relations with owners and stakeholder groups.

Skill at handling expectations is thus one of the first competencies that a person must have in order to manage a transition successfully. How do some executives succeed in managing the abundance of often inflated expectations while steadfastly charting their own course? Are there any typical expectations attached to a change in leadership, or is each change in leadership unique? Which expectations should be taken seriously and which not? Where do expectations come from and how can they be managed proactively?

The *expectations of superiors* are a rather problematic matter for new managers. When I advise managers, I ask immediately what they think their superiors expect of them in the new job. The answers are usually pretty sketchy. Surprisingly, such an important event as filling a leadership position is often precisely when expectations fail to be spelled out – despite all the calls for clear objectives. If anything at all is explained, the executives focus on the usual quantitative objectives, mentioning more sales, better variable gross margin, and lower costs as important expectations. Pre-eminent expectations such as supporting a superior's own work or ensuring loyalty are rarely voiced. They are taken for granted and discussed only if they are not met. Executives often simply make too little time for them, contenting themselves with only a brief talk with their new manager and generally not preparing sufficiently even for that.

In order to avoid appearing 'insecure' from the outset, new managers usually forgo the chance to specify expectations, making misunderstandings inevitable. Many managers fail to ask about the simplest things, such as important milestones and the criteria for success in their new position. These omissions are all the more serious when managers come from a different area or even a different company. In those cases they usually confine their negotiations to contractual conditions and their prospects for the future.

Expectations

What are the three most important goals of your boss?

What has been done to achieve those goals in the past two years?

Explanations

What explanations does your boss have for not having achieved the stated goals?

How much do the explanations of the employees differ from the assessments by senior managers?

What expectations do the employees, customers and suppliers have of you according to your boss?

What do senior managers think is most critical to your success: the trust of your employees, the relation to a few key players, or the relation to customers and suppliers?

Relations

What changes of personnel and positions have already taken place as part of the change in leadership?

Who do your senior managers think is going to feel sidelined?

Who has been actively involved in tackling the transition phase thus far?

Who has been consulted on important decisions?

Figure 2 What you should know before assuming your new position

THE EXPECTATIONS OF THE EMPLOYEES

The expectations entertained by the employees seem much clearer at first glance. They often come right out with their expectations and hopes: 'You're here at last! The first thing you have to do is solve the problem that we're understaffed', 'What we urgently need is new PCs' or 'You have such a good line to the field organization, so maybe you can see to it that they work better with us.' You get a load of problems at the very beginning, especially if you are touted as the saviour of a team that is having trouble.

But even employees talk openly about only some of the expectations. The ones most likely to be formulated clearly are those pertaining to the solution of old problems. Improved flow of information, greater team spirit and more constructive collaboration are some of the perennial topics that are quick to be identified.

Employees are much less forthcoming in stating their personal expectations. Not until the newcomer patiently asks the employees what they hope their manager can do for them will they articulate the otherwise unstated expectations of personal security and advancement. As we have observed during consulting assignments, employees are concerned about certain matters. 'Will the new person succeed at improving the working climate?' 'Will I get a better chance for professional development?' 'Will the new manager represent us better to the outside world?' These questions are the ones on an employee's mind, though they are not always expressed.

THE EXPECTATIONS OF COLLEAGUES

Stated as well as implicit (and therefore unstated) expectations are a characteristic part of leadership transitions. That is why it is crucial to listen not only to the explicit expectations but also to those hiding 'between the lines'. In fact, successful managers in new positions listen in every direction for what is not said, as hidden expectations have an easily underestimated potential as a source of resistance to change and as criteria for the evaluation of a new manager's success.

John Snow was new in the company. He came from a competitor known for its progressive sales and distribution concept. Part of his job as head of marketing was to develop new ways of 'getting sales going'. He had set off on a tour of the regions and had developed a host of ideas. They jelled into a concept in detailed discussions with his boss, who had likewise moved into this job just two years earlier.

'I simply don't know what the matter with them is! When I presented a few of my ideas in our last meeting, my colleagues, the regional sales directors, were totally reserved. My colleague from advertising did not show much support, either. And I was still being very cautious with my proposals.'

What happened? Something quite typical. John had energetically attacked his new duties, gathered information and kept his boss fully informed. But he had forgotten two things:

- His boss had not been around all that long himself and thus did not yet enjoy the confidence of all the managers.

- Colleagues always respond coolly when a newcomer presents new ideas too vigorously. They fear that their past work is being undervalued.

In his local discussions, John had failed to enquire thoroughly about successful initiatives in the past. He had focused much too quickly on everything that could be done differently. After all, he had a favourite comparison in the company he used to work for.

Colleagues expect a newcomer to ask about *their* rules of the game, not to present new ideas too quickly, and to avoid forging too close an alliance with the powers that be. They assume that the newcomer will come to them, not the other way around. John Snow could have made it easier for himself by finding out in his conversations what had contributed to the company's success thus far. Then, if he had conveyed an appreciation of his colleagues' past work in the presentation of his ideas, he would certainly have garnered more spontaneous support.

The boss's expectations:

- Do as I would do.

- Be quick.

- Be loyal.

- Support me in my position.

Employees' expectations:

- Solve our problems without us having to do much for it.

- Show us that you too are not perfect.

- Let us keep our positions.

- See to our development.

Colleagues' expectations:

- Bring in new ideas without devaluing our work.

- Respect our achievements.

- Don't ally yourself against us.

- Inform yourself about our rules of the game.

Figure 3 Unstated expectations attached to a change in leadership

EXPECTATIONS ENTAILED IN TAKING OVER A MANAGERIAL POSITION IN A FOREIGN COUNTRY

When change occurs at a foreign site, expectations acquire a totally different meaning. Sometimes the newcomer runs up against a wall of ingrained images and preconceived notions about headquarters and foreign people. There is unspoken resentment around, for example, 'Someone from headquarters is coming in again' or 'How often do we have to break in foreign people?'

Because these expectations are often even less directly articulated abroad than at home, and may even be altogether impossible to express because of language barriers, it takes entirely different procedures to clarify expectations. When a manager is operating in a different country, obtaining a precise picture requires seeking out many more people's perspectives than would be needed in a transition at home. In some countries, moreover, the expectations confronting the newcomer stem from stakeholder groups that are different from those the manager is accustomed to dealing with. In addition, the interaction with political stakeholders varies from country to country.

When trying to spell out expectations, though, it is paramount that one is careful not to rely solely on the accounts of other expatriate managers. Many of them have a limited picture and are keener to find an ally than to portray the different perspectives objectively. It is also helpful to become thoroughly acquainted with the history of the local operation. A new manager should obtain as much information as possible about the background of the company situation in order to decode the expectations others hold, especially if culturally conditioned reticence impedes open and frank communication.

DEVELOP EXPECTATIONS ACTIVELY

The expectations of employees, superiors and colleagues are important. So are the expectations of neighbouring departments, employee representatives and predecessors who have been promoted. It is important to ask not only about explicit expectations but also about those that are not expressed.

1. Who sent me and what is my official mission?

2. What are people saying about me and this new assignment in the host country?

3. What do my immediate superiors expect?

4. What do my new employees expect?

5. What history does this site have with expatriates?

6. Who ultimately made the decision to send an expatriate for this job?

7. Are there hidden competitors for the position I am filling?

8. What does the site need from me or my function?

Figure 4 Questions to clarify expectations in an international assignment

I am often asked whether it is not dangerous to ask too much about expectations. After all, there is the risk of raising hopes that cannot be met. However, expectations don't go away by being ignored. They have a habit of staying on. At best they turn into support for the changes to come; at worst they harbour the potential for resistance to the new executive's plans. Neither should be ignored.

You should ask key players the following questions:

Have these expectations been around for a while?

Who else has these expectations?

Are any other expectations tied to this one?

What are other departments likely to expect from our department?

If this particular expectation were met, what would be the likely result?

Why do you expect this specifically from me?

Figure 5 Actively explore expectations

This is such a key learning point for managers making the transition into a new role that I would like to take a brief look at the logic of expectations. What does *expect* mean anyway? What is behind expectations and how can they best be dealt with?

- Expectations are *desires, ideas, hopes, suggested solutions to problems,* and *recommendations.* They are neither programmes to fulfil nor responsibilities to meet. On the contrary, if I were to ask employees about their expectations and tell them that each stated expectation would immediately become a programme, I would receive few answers. In this sense, expectations are just views and ideas, which, however, give superb insight into the thinking of the people being asked. They are also the perspectives by which my own action is judged.

You must therefore know what the expectations are. This is the only way to keep from flying blind and to know how your action is being appraised.

- Expectations are *not logical*. They are frequently a mix of contradictory emotional desires and matter-of-fact proposals for solving problems.

  You therefore have to differentiate between expectations and explore what lies behind them.

- Expectations stand for a basic attitude – waiting. 'Let's see whether he [she] succeeds at it' is a sentence frequently heard in changes of leadership. Lurking behind it is the passivity of wait-and-see. That is why expectations have to be translated into tasks.

  You therefore have to ask which expectations can be turned into shared tasks.

Now take some time and consider who wants what from you. If you find that you just do not know what is expected of you from different directions, then think of it as a trigger to seek a focused discussion. The checklist in Figure 6 will help you structure your thinking, and Figure 7 summarizes the key learning points from Building Block 1.

1. What do senior managers/your boss expect of you?
Openly stated:
Unstated:

2. What do your employees expect of you?
Openly stated:
Unstated:

3. What do your colleagues expect of you?
Openly stated:
Unstated:

4. What do your customers expect of you?
Openly stated:
Unstated:

5. What does your predecessor expect of you?
Openly stated:
Unstated:

6. What does your family expect of you?
Openly stated:
Unstated:

7. What do you expect of yourself?
Openly stated:
Unstated:

8. Which expectations do you want to examine more
   closely?

_____

_____

_____

Figure 6 Checklist: stated and unstated expectations from different directions

1. Proactively seek out the expectations of different groups of people. Ask senior managers, employees, colleagues and customers. Consider the stated expectations as ideas and perspectives for shaping your own strategy.

2. Dig below the surface to understand what is behind the expectations. Ask what the expectations mean, how urgent they are and who shares them.

3. In discussions and meetings, explore expectations that can be developed into joint tasks. However, do not take this as permission to push ahead with your own ideas and strategy.

Some typical mistakes to avoid:

- considering expectations as responsibilities that must be met immediately;
- neglecting colleagues' expectations of respect and recognition;
- forgetting your employees' expectations of stability and security.

Figure 7 Summary of Building Block 1

Building Block 2

Developing the key relationships

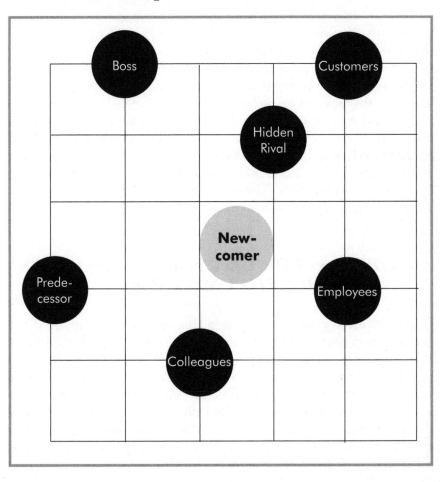

Most changes in leadership run aground on the shoals of the key relationships.

Carly Fiorina, former CEO of Hewlett-Packard, was once thought to be the most powerful businesswoman in the United States. But even she failed to see the significance of a solid relationship with the Hewlett family. Instead she promised 'revolution' and to do away with the consensus culture so characteristic of the company. During the acquisition of Compaq she ignored their opposition. When difficulties emerged, the old resistance did too, and one factor that sped up her downfall was public opposition of Hewlett family members, which added to the official reason of irreconcilable differences in opinion about the strategic direction of the company (*Frankfurter Allgemeine Zeitung*, 10 February 2005, No. 34, p. 19).

In many instances, relations with shareholders, superiors, employees, clients and colleagues decide the success of a change in leadership. Misunderstandings and lack of clarity in important relationships are liable to lead to tensions that are difficult, if not impossible, to compensate for in the difficult phase of assuming a new position. If disappointed rivals or hidden competitors block the new manager, the task can easily become overwhelming.

'But who do I need to watch out for? Which are the key players I must attend to?' 'How do I deal with hidden rivals and informal leaders?' 'What contacts do I need in order to put important changes into motion?' 'What do I need to find out from my boss so that I can take action successfully?' These are the questions that occupy, and should occupy, anyone moving into a new position.

ON DEALING WITH DISAPPOINTED RIVALS AND HIDDEN COMPETITORS

Quite simply, key relationships in a change of leadership are those relationships that are important to taking over a position successfully. The problem is that it is usually easier to determine after the fact which ones were key and which were not.

One primary player, of course, is the person who managed things while the position was vacant. Not only do the employees think of the person as having carried out the responsibilities that the newcomer will assume, but the interim manager has claims on the position of leadership, whether or not he or she admits it.

Garrison Sands, head of a research unit in a major company, is a typical example of what happens in such cases. He is 42 and has been with the company for eight years, having come from a university where he had already directed international research projects. He is a specialist in his field and was specially sought out by the company. A year ago, his boss, the head of the research unit, died unexpectedly. Garrison was asked to assume this responsibility because he was thought to have not only the necessary technical competence but also considerable leadership skills. From the outset, though, he was also told that the arrangement should in no way be taken to mean that he had a claim on the senior position. On the contrary, negotiations with a successor were already under way, and it was hoped that the post could be filled in just a few months.

Things turned out differently. The position was vacant for more than a year because the discussions mentioned at the beginning broke down very quickly. Garrison was not at all happy about the outcome at first, for he neither saw a chance of winning the position himself nor had he a great interest in doing so. His ongoing projects demanded a great deal of him as a specialist and were important enough to absorb him fully. He was often torn between research and management duties and strove to accomplish both.

A year is a long time. His initial reserve in the management committee meetings passed, and he championed his research area actively and combatively, as was his nature. Month by month, without realizing it, he gradually came to terms with his role as interim director. He began to identify more and more with his management duties and often caught himself asking whether this position was the right one for him in the long run.

Top management's announcement that someone had finally been found to succeed the boss who had died a year earlier came as a blow to Garrison. He was indignant, sceptical and furious with his superiors, who had relied on him for so long. The employees, too, reacted angrily, for after their initial scepticism they had adjusted to him. True, he could not fault top management, for they had never said anything other than that a successor was being sought. Nevertheless, he was deeply disappointed, a reaction that led him to be extremely critical towards the new manager.

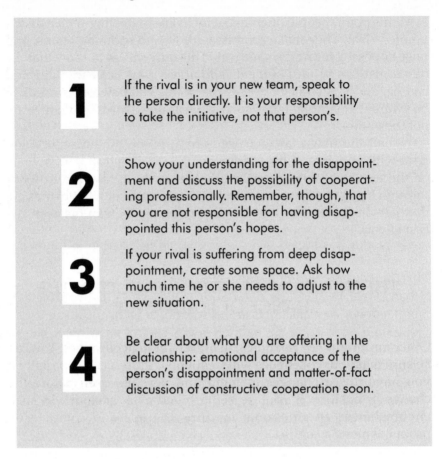

Figure 8 Dealing with disappointed rivals

It would be a mistake to give a hidden rival the cold shoulder during a change in leadership. Trouble would develop very quickly not only with that person but also with the employees, who would then side with the rival. He or she wants to be talked to and asked for advice. Show understanding for the person's disappointment and discuss rationally the possibilities for cooperating professionally. You must realize, however, that the rival's disappointment is not your fault.

At this point, people often make mistakes in dealing with a disappointed rival. They make promises, try to find soothing words, and raise hopes for future perspectives. This only serves to show that the newcomer has no idea of the disappointed rival's true thinking and feeling, and this strategy misses the point. The newcomer needs to be aware that simple things such as promises, words and hopes are not the issue.

Instead the new manager needs to approach the disappointed rival with understanding and the dispassionate question of how he or she envisions future cooperation. It is the rival's job to work through his or her disappointment. Your contribution lies in making that person a fair offer and thereby bridging the gap between the two of you.

THE SIGNIFICANCE OF COLLEAGUES IN THE CHANGE OF LEADERSHIP

Other important key relations are found among colleagues. You can be sure that your colleagues will treat you with reserve, especially if you have major changes in mind and perhaps even before the change of position if you are being billed as a 'saviour'. In such circumstances an emotional mixture of hope and competition produces many a conflict.

The dynamics of such conflicts are well illustrated by the example of a young sales director assigned to build up a new business area in a large company. Of course, there were rivals, but they were not the problem. No one envied him his task, for he had to gain a footing in quite a tough market segment. He came from outside and knew the market but not the company's internal structures. Then something typical occurred, but for him it was quite dangerous: the development of a new sales line absorbed him so much that he threw himself totally into the task. He looked after his employees and the progress of the new organizational structure.

He designed marketing concepts and negotiated with important clients. He could handle everything only by working 80 hours a week.

After six months he was supposed to give the first thorough presentation of his concept at a conference. At the same time, he canvassed his colleagues to support him in the expansion of his business by naming possible customers. To his surprise he encountered nothing but great resistance. His colleagues critically questioned the solidity of his success and recommended that he first examine his concepts somewhat more closely. He then became completely incensed when his boss, with whom he had discussed the strategy beforehand, did not support him as he had hoped either.

He was furious when he came to our coaching session. He was enraged with his colleagues and his superiors, and did not seem to understand anything about what was unfolding. 'After all, they brought me in to rebuild this business,' he commented, 'and promised to back me in every way. Now when I need that support, they stab me in the back.'

When I asked him when he had spoken to his colleagues about his strategy, he continued angrily: 'I have better things to do than run around the place. My colleagues can do that.'

Slowly but surely, his wrath subsided, and I succeeded in getting him interested in the perspectives of his colleagues. I asked what he already knew about their activities, what connections there were between his strategies and their dealings, and what areas his activities could even be a threat to. He had to admit that he had given little thought to those things thus far.

You may well deplore this kind of problem in companies. The fact is that feelings play a central part in our organizations no matter how much we swear by objectivity and rationality. When leadership changes and a shift occur, in the intricate web of important roles and relationships at work emotions acquire special significance. The disappointment felt by hidden rivals, and the offence that colleagues take at the ideas of the newcomer are almost always denied, but they determine how well the new manager is able to establish him- or herself in the new environment.

Successful managers in new positions are masters at the game of relationships. They know about hidden levels of feelings and take them into consideration when taking action. More or less intuitively, they develop strategies with which they accommodate emotional wishes and yet also make objective demands. They go directly to their colleagues and ask them about their expectations. These managers draw on colleagues as an important source of knowledge about the company and thereby pave the way for successful implementation of the changes they have in mind.

THE PREDECESSOR – THE HIDDEN COMPETITION

The relationship to a predecessor is a special topic in the subject of leadership transition. The matter goes beyond relations between the newcomer and the predecessor to include those with the employees too, because they will always compare the two bosses with each other – 'Let's just see if he [she] does it better' or 'We've heard *that* before.' In other words, they create an underlying dynamic of competition. This dynamic is well illustrated by what happened at the German computer company Nixdorf. No matter what Klaus Luft did, he had almost no chance. Virtually everything he did was compared with the actions of his glorified predecessor, Heinz Nixdorf, and was, hence, more or less openly devalued.

This mechanism, which at least temporarily accords successors little opportunity to do anything better than their admired predecessors, comes to bear especially when the mistakes of one's predecessor become apparent. To shield an esteemed former boss, those who used to surround him or her project on to the newcomer all the problems that surface, claiming 'We would have found a better solution to this earlier.'

Glorified predecessors are not the only ones who are difficult to follow. Openly criticized predecessors are a particularly persistent burden for newcomers, because employees hope you will save the day. 'You're here at last', they think to themselves. Imagine being repeatedly confronted with 'everything that went wrong earlier' and with 'everything that should have been done differently'. It is not always easy to keep the necessary distance from the performance of your predecessor, especially when you discover real errors the person made and when you have to face critical comments from customers. But beware. Don't make the mistake of accepting the invitation to complain about your predecessor's possible weaknesses, for then you will experience fully the double nature of the situation. Faster than you can think, the employees will about-face and brief you on the former boss's merits!

The balance between criticism and loyalty is highly erratic when it comes to employees' memory of their former boss. It is affected when the newcomer agrees with critical statements. The attitude swings immediately toward loyalty. The new boss is then no longer seen as a saviour but rather as someone who can't keep from mud-slinging.

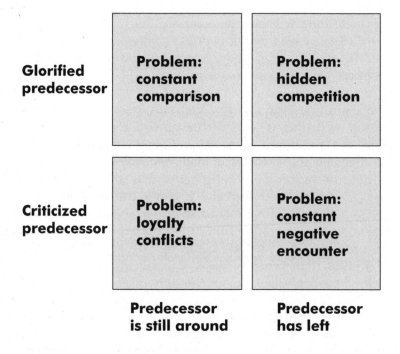

Figure 9 The impact of predecessors

Another, no less difficult, quandary involving the predecessor arises when that person is still active in the company. The dynamics depend heavily on what position the predecessor has taken. Things are usually simpler if he or she has been promoted. But if the employees feel that their former boss got a raw deal from top management, then your predecessor will continue to enjoy the loyalty of the employees and you will not have an easy time of it.

What if the promoted predecessor is now your boss? You then have to deal not only with the difficulty of the predecessor letting go but also with the constant comparison by the employees. After all, at least some of the people who used to report to your boss now report to you. Clear agreements and efficient transition rituals are essential in this set-up (see Building Block 7). Absolutely clear signals are needed so everyone recognizes the authority of the new manager.

Figure 10 presents a number of questions to which you should know the answers so that you can protect yourself from hidden competition with your predecessor.

1. In what way(s) are you different from your predecessor?

2. Which difference is important to you?

3. How can you explain this difference without saying that your predecessor made a mistake?

4. In what area was your predecessor perhaps better than you?

5. If your predecessor were still in the department, what would he or she definitely not agree with?

Figure 10 Checklist: a few questions to help you avoid unnecessary competition with your predecessor

INVITATIONS BETTER REFUSED

'Either you or me!' or 'You have to show us first whether you can do that' or 'You really can do that better than your predecessor' or 'Finally someone can tell us how we can get better organized.' These statements are 'invitations' heard in many leadership transitions. They are more or less overtly formulated recommendations that, if accepted by the newcomer, will lead to serious trouble. The moment you buy into the viewpoint lurking behind these invitations, you meet the negative expectations. For example, if you engage with the disappointed rival in an 'either you or me' mode, which can be very difficult to avoid when such employees try hard to provoke you, you are making a major mistake. The predictable response is: 'You see, I told you right away that he [she] wants to get rid of me!' Such cases are liable to degenerate into vicious circles of self-fulfilling prophecies.

These dynamics are not confined to disappointed rivals. My experience is that they often develop between a team and the new leader. The risk is particularly high when a team has been working very effectively, perhaps even for a long period, without formal leadership. In such cases the team's attitude toward the newcomer can be quite challenging, and may signal 'It's up to you to prove that we need you.'

When a team closes ranks, the new leader risks triggering a vicious circle if he or she talks about previous experience in resolving issues. It is equally dangerous in such situations for the new leader immediately to start attending team meetings. Admittedly, probably one of the most difficult things to endure as a leader is to hear 'You are not needed.' The all-too-human reaction to this challenge is to force the issue, but such an approach is the wrong one.

Seasoned new managers practise patience in such instances. They know that the employees need some time to accept that they are no longer alone and must relinquish some of the authority they had previously exercised on their own. Experienced managers also know that it is only a question of time until constant challenges will give them the opportunity to take action. Meanwhile, they confine themselves to gathering information, making contacts and performing typical managerial duties. They ask the teams to take part in calling on customers and to attend meetings, and they ensure follow-through. Above all, they also find out what works well so that the team does not get the impression that their new head wants to break up the obviously efficient structures.

Being cast in the position of the classic 'knight in shining armour' is equally problematic, though it looks simpler than taking the lead of a well-functioning team. If a team has been waiting for the newcomer's highly praised management talent, accepting the invitation to show it off is one of the biggest mistakes that the manager can make. 'What should we do?' 'The best thing for you to do is...' Experience shows that such an approach cements the actors in their roles of the saviour and the weak. The situation becomes increasingly unhealthy because the new manager is soon at a loss to know where support is needed next, and the team feels increasingly incapable. After a while, the manager wonders why resistance is mounting. What is happening is what Warren Bennis in the 1980s referred to as 'the unconscious conspiracy waged by organizations against their leaders'. One form of that conspiracy becomes apparent when the team starts seeking to break out of its apparent weakness and incompetence by seeing to it that the recommendations of the 'knight in shining armour' no longer work.

This mechanism's effect escalates still further if cultural differences come into play. At that point it is especially crucial for a new expatriate manager to refrain from giving rash advice, because the foreign person's way of doing things is likely to be rejected. One of the typical problems of the expatriate situation is the tension between expatriate managers who believe that only their knowledge and experience will help and employees whose experience with other expatriates leads them to fear that *their* knowledge once again does not count. The Golden Rule to follow in such leadership transitions in a new culture is to gather as much information as you can about the special features of the situation and its background, to be curious and open to cues, and to trust in the resources of the employees.

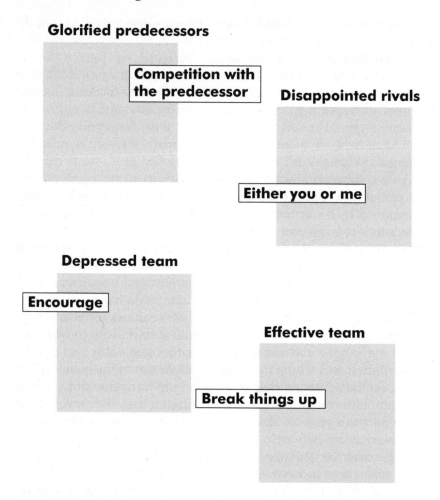

Figure 11 Invitations you would be better off not accepting

NETWORKING – DEVELOPING POWER AND INFLUENCE

Developing key relationships means identifying the key players and dealing with the feelings of loyalty, competition and disappointment that are so typical of leadership transition processes. This is not enough, however. Developing key relationships also means judiciously building a powerful network.

Anyone wanting to move things forward, as Jeffrey Pfeffer persuasively described in his book *Power in Organizations*, must gain power and influence. Managers must have contacts that enable them to appraise the political currents in the company and to secure the necessary support for carrying out their plans. Powerful networks are pivotal, because most projects in companies today require the backing of people over whom you have no direct influence. The power of your position does not help much in such situations. For example, if you want to convince your colleagues in product management that your new marketing strategy is worth pursuing, the decisions required for it have to be carefully prepared.

How do you develop power and influence in organizations in order to drive the things forward that you believe are important? You have to know who is a central figure in crucial decisions, who usually has the right to veto action, and who is often the sceptic. You must know who should be informed before meetings and where important informal groups are that discuss the decisions in advance. You must also be able to assess how the forces of stability and change are distributed and where the lines of power run in the company. In this respect the manager making a leadership transition from within the organization no doubt has advantages that the new leader coming in from outside does not have. The insider knows more about the relevant networks in the company. But insiders, too, must ask themselves the questions in the checklist in Figure 12.

Only when you succeed in making yourself an active part of the network of relationships that exist beyond the formal organization chart do you have a realistic chance of initiating relatively big changes. Above all, you will have a chance of seeing them through to completion. Networking, the focused and systematic development of an influential network of relationships, is an important resource especially for processes of restructuring or strategic reorientation.

1. Whose cooperation will I need to achieve what I am striving for?

2. What will be their standpoints, and what will they probably think of my intentions?

3. Who will delay or sidetrack what I am trying to do? Who will be affected by what I am striving to do and therefore seek to thwart my intentions?

4. What is my base for gaining power and influence? How can I expand this base in order to support my decision?

5. What relationships must I cultivate in order to be informed quickly enough about events in the company?

Figure 12 Checklist: a few questions about developing power and influence

1. Ask about rivals and the whereabouts of your predecessor and other people who played key roles in the past in order to assess the emotional side of your starting position.

2. Proactively approach the emotionally affected employees, colleagues and superiors. They expect the newcomer to come to them, not vice versa.

3. Avoid the invitations typical of leadership transitions. Bear in mind the hidden competition with your predecessor and your team.

4. Systematically develop your network of relationships that ensure your influence. Don't let work on your task keep you from investing time in relationships. You will regret it later.

Some typical mistakes to avoid:

- giving disappointed rivals the cold shoulder;
- criticizing your predecessor's performance;
- trying to impress your employees with the knowledge and experience you bring from previous assignments;
- regarding conversations with colleagues as a leisure activity;
- concentrating exclusively on your work.

Figure 13 Summary of Building Block 2

Building Block 3

Constructively analysing the initial situation

Perspective 1

Rules and culture

- The social architecture of the organization
- Rules, assumptions and stories

Perspective 2

The issues

- Tractable and intractable issues
- Urgent and less urgent issues
- Persistent issues

Perspective 3

The facts

- Results
- Strategies
- Costs
- Mishaps and complaints

Perspective 4

Innovative potential

- Willingness to change
- Know-how about change
- Climate for change

Perspective 5

The resources

- Strengths in leadership, culture, organization, power and technology

As strange as it may sound, the fact is that trouble may well be just around the corner if you attack problems as soon as they are brought to your attention. If you forge ahead without trying to find out what has already been done to find a solution to the problems, you may end up having a great deal to do without necessarily succeeding at it.

In his book *The Logic of Failure*, Dietrich Dörner, a German specialist in the psychology of thinking, describes how people actually ensure failure. He put trained macroeconomists, physicists and managers in front of a computer and confronted them with typical contemporary leadership tasks. For example, they were instructed to cope with a drought in an African country. In another exercise the participants took the role of mayors whose task was to lead a town into a prosperous future. The special thing about this experiment was that Dörner's computers were able to simulate the development of the situation and the long-term effects of the decisions taken by the participants.

The results were both alarming and instructive. They gave deep insight into Western habits of thinking, planning and decision making. The typical mistakes that separated the successful from the less successful 'mayors' were: 1) the failure to consider long-term impacts and side effects, 2) misassessments of how things develop in a situation, 3) inappropriate distinctions between important and unimportant factors, and 4) rash acceptance of hypotheses as truths requiring no further examination. The participants who felt emotional pressure because they noticed that they could indeed act but did not know the outcomes often resorted to taking action blindly.

As Dörner noted, such responses are not much different to those in real life. Just open the newspaper and see how top business executives and government leaders try with varying degrees of success to master the complexity of modern times. 'The problem is', Dörner explained, 'that we live today in a world of interacting subsystems in which people also have to think in interacting subsystems.' In most cases, leadership transition may not be as complex a task as that of governing a town, with its nearly unimaginable number of interdependent factors. But they are not much simpler either. Leadership transitions likewise are bound to entail a multitude of interacting factors if the process of taking over a position is to stay on course. Another typical feature of situations in which classic Western, linear, cause–effect thinking proves misleading is that many of the variables are not immediately visible. A characteristic of leadership transitions is that the newcomer must not only come to grips with a host of issues and problems but also make decisions without being thoroughly informed at all. As we know today, complex, dynamic and opaque situations call for special approaches. It is not a matter of attempting a complete analysis of the situation. Nor is it about analysing the weak points, for that only triggers a witch-hunt that destroys the climate for change.

What you need is *views*. Engineers use this word to refer to a procedure they often use when they are certain that an all-inclusive analysis of the situation is not possible. The crucial factor in this procedure is not the degree of detail and depth of the analysis but rather the choice of views. Engineers ensure that they have as sharp a picture of the situation as possible by modelling it from different perspectives.

Many managers in new positions tend to focus on too few views. Some newcomers thus attack the *problems* and want to know exactly what was done wrong. Others concentrate on the *facts* and design new strategies based only on them. In many coaching sessions, our job is to broaden the views of the managers systematically. In doing so, we have brought some surprising knowledge to the surface.

Five perspectives have proved particularly useful for analysing the situation the new manager faces at the outset of the transition process:

- Perspective 1: the rules and assumptions guiding the people involved;
- Perspective 2: the issues occupying the organization;
- Perspective 3: the facts that determine action;
- Perspective 4: the available potential for innovation;
- Perspective 5: the resources on which you can build.

DISCOVER THE CORPORATE CULTURE

There are *hard* and *soft* realities. In companies, spheres of responsibility, the organization chart, numbers and strategies are among the hard realities. The identification of the employees with their company, their willingness to change, and the quality of communication are traditionally called soft realities. Surprisingly, as any seasoned manager will confirm, the purportedly hard realities are easier and quicker to change than the so-called soft corporate culture.

Perhaps that is why so much more attention has been paid in recent decades to the soft side of the organization than to its hard side. Peters and Waterman's classic, *In Search of Excellence,* captured key messages about the power of organizational culture. Based on their analysis of successful US businesses, they came to the remarkable realization that it was not the efficiency of methods or management strategies that accounted for the greater profitability of these companies compared with their competitors. On the contrary, in many cases their success was due to nothing more than a handful of simple goals and messages. The essential difference between these companies and less successful ones was that those goals and messages were deeply shared and supported by all the employees. In a now widely known model, Peters and Waterman then took the soft factors of motivation, enthusiasm, customer orientation and quality and juxtaposed them with the traditionally hard factors such as structure, strategy and system.

'Corporate culture', as noted by Ulrich Weber, probably one of the most acclaimed experts on such matters, 'has become a first-order factor of competition.'

You, too, should therefore begin your analysis of the initial situation by exploring the rules, assumptions and values that underpin the way people think and work in your new department. Take advantage of being the person who 'still sees everything with new eyes'. Be attentive, and you will learn a great deal about the organization in your first days, especially if you have had little contact with the new area until now or have come from a different company.

Successful managers soak up the new organization and its culture like a sponge. They listen to the words people use, ask about the rules and observe habits. They hear stories and learn who has or has had a major influence on the area. They also watch and carefully note the way criticism and mistakes are dealt with and the way people comment on the customers and company image.

Slowly but surely, an initial picture of the new organization forms. You begin to see its social architecture, albeit often only sketchily at first. You come to discover how the employees think about the company and how they see its mission. You recognize whether the corporate image presented in the glossy brochures is actually lived in the organization. You learn whether the employees see their task only as difficult or also as stimulating. Basic attitudes towards power, the handling of information and the ability to innovate are key elements of the corporate culture (see Figure 14).

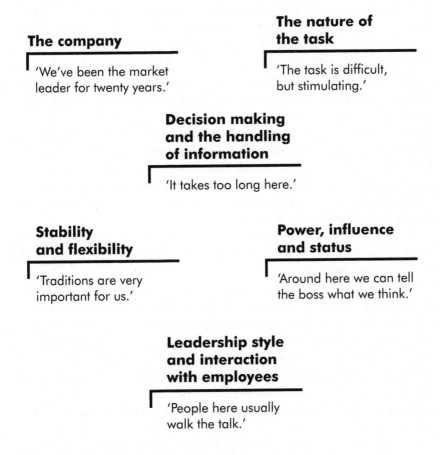

The company

'We've been the market leader for twenty years.'

The nature of the task

'The task is difficult, but stimulating.'

Decision making and the handling of information

'It takes too long here.'

Stability and flexibility

'Traditions are very important for us.'

Power, influence and status

'Around here we can tell the boss what we think.'

Leadership style and interaction with employees

'People here usually walk the talk.'

Figure 14 The social architecture of a company

1. How do the employees talk about the company or their department?

2. What habits did you notice in your first days on the job?

3. What stories were told to you first? Which people were introduced to you as important?

4. Who communicates with whom? Who does not communicate with whom?

5. Are there striking communication habits such as interrupting, criticizing or refusing to discuss problems?

6. How do the employees talk about customers and other departments?

7. Who has information and how is it handled?

8. What is the significance of status and power?

9. What is the mood?

10. How are successes explained? How are difficulties explained?

11. Are there corporate principles? How are they dealt with?

Figure 15 Checklist: observations in the new department

SORT THROUGH THE ISSUES

The second thing you must identify is what the issues are that preoccupy people in the organization. You have to know what your supervisor thinks should be dealt with urgently and what hopes your employees pin on your arrival. The views of other departments and of customers on the problems that need to be solved are also necessary information for you in getting your bearings.

It is important not to regard the list of problems as anything other than a description of the situation from various perspectives. One of the biggest mistakes you can make is to treat the description of problems as objective fact. The descriptions of the situations always reflect the describer's interests, values and ideas for solutions.

If members of the sales team say that the most urgent problems are to ensure support from other departments in the company, improve sales concepts and change the pricing, that is correct – in their view. It is correct when the boss states that the most important task for the new regional director is to 'form a team'. That is the boss's description and personal perspective on things, and it reflects his or her experience that optimal performance is achievable only in a team.

Gather as much information as possible. The more descriptions of the situation you collect and the more definitions of problems you hear, the better. They fill out your picture of the situation and can help you to identify possible issues. In this phase, however, you should also begin to distinguish between them:

- Ask your employees how they would rank the issues.

- Ask which issues are interlinked and what your employees think the customers see as the most urgent issues to resolve.

- Ask what problems they think can be solved with resources the company already has, and make sure that you also ask whether these problems have been around a long time.

- Ask what has already been tried and why no lasting solution has been found yet.

Issue	How long has it been around?	Past attempts to solve it
1.		
2.		
3.		
4.		
5.		

Figure 16 Checklist: persistent issues in the new department

You will be surprised in more ways than one! Nearly 80 per cent of the problems you are told about at the beginning are persistent ones. In other words, they are issues that people over the years have already found to be hard nuts to crack.

I well remember a director of development who suddenly became aware of the mistake he had just made as I lectured in a seminar about perpetual issues. He, too, had asked around in his department about problems and 'weak points' and was told about many. One problem was especially impressed on him: the constant interruption of 'real' development work by the short-term problems of customers. He had just begun to take on this problem when my comment made it clear that this issue was a perennial one. Many things had been tried, but every effort in recent years had failed to solve the matter. The customers, who often brought their issues to top management, always received highest priority in the end.

Let there be no misunderstanding: persistent issues are not insoluble! The solution to such problems just takes considerable and, above all, *joint* effort. The question of when and how to address an issue of this sort needs to be carefully weighed.

GATHER THE FACTS

Apart from knowing rules, understanding the culture and identifying old and new issues, you must know the facts. It is a third perspective from which you can illuminate the initial situation. You must know what the results or profit contributions are. You must find out where the costs arise and what efforts have been taken thus far to cut them. You need figures on the status of the various products or services on the market, and you need information about the organization's strategy. You must patiently and consistently ask about who actually works with whom and which interfaces regularly involve problems. Get someone to provide or create an overview of the frequency of particular breakdowns or complaints.

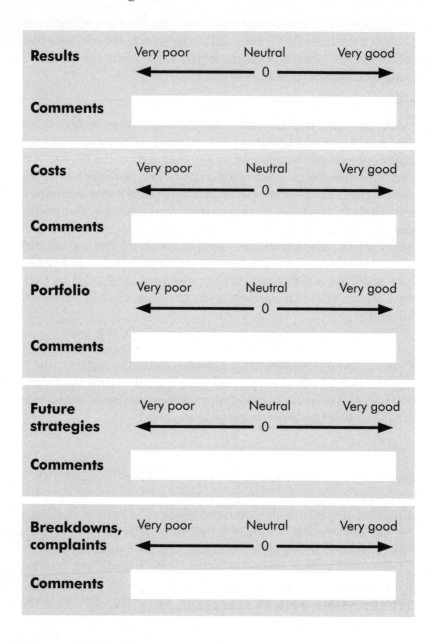

Figure 17 Gathering the facts

An interesting contradiction between the descriptions of the soft problems and the hard facts usually emerges. Hard and soft do not mean better or worse. They are a pair of opposites necessary for gaining as complete a picture of things as possible.

> While advising the payment transaction department of a bank, we achieved a surprising change in perspective by juxtaposing the staff's complaints and a few facts. The members of this department had long been very dissatisfied. They complained about their working conditions, their status in the company and the lack of interest in their problems. In their eyes, convincing evidence that they were right lay in the forms their own colleagues filled out at the counters. These forms were said to be filled out so poorly that they were a major reason for the work delays that led to the customary stress of closing accounts on Fridays as legally required. All discussions with the colleagues at the counters had reportedly led nowhere.
>
> Conducting a detailed analysis, we asked the staff in the payment transaction department to list more precisely how many forms were incompletely filled out. The surprising realization was that these documents constituted only a small percentage of the workload. There were numerous other sources of stress that needed addressing much more urgently.

Consultants frequently encounter such examples in their work. It is not a matter of using the facts to wipe the complaints off the table. It is simply a matter of making the tension between soft and hard factors apparent. That is how new approaches and ideas emerge as a possible solution to the problems.

DETERMINE THE POTENTIAL FOR INNOVATION

Whenever it comes to solving problems and getting your bearings on a constantly changing market situation, willingness to change is also involved. Flexibility, the ability to learn and the willingness to make even profound structural change are therefore among the most valued organizational characteristics in business today.

It has long been known that cultures differ in both their willingness and their ability to innovate. Rolf Berth, the director of the Kienbaum Forum for Innovation, has given German companies a dismal report card. According to him, too much unquestioning belief in authority, too little willingness to take risks, and a concentration on weaknesses are leading to a systematic decline in innovation in German companies. Often, potential is not even the trouble; it has much more to do with bureaucratic structures.

It is repeatedly the same company structures that nip new ideas in the bud. 'Quite interesting; go ahead and work it out sometime' and 'We have to attend to business at the moment' are two stock sentences of a culture hostile to innovation. Nicholas Hayek, known for reviving the Swiss watchmaking industry with his Swatch, states that companies tend to become willing to take risks only when business is no longer going well. According to him, the banks would not have supported his crazy watch project if the two watch companies that he bought had not been deep in the red for years.

1. Confidence in own abilities.

2. Forward-looking perspective.

3. Open communication even on mistakes and failures.

4. Ability to perceive and celebrate successes.

5. Respect for different experiences and viewpoints.

6. Long-term orientation.

7. Patience and flexibility.

Figure 18 Features of a positive climate for change

Other companies, too, such as Hewlett-Packard and 3M, show that things can work differently. They consistently promote innovative performance by their employees, constantly monitor innovative projects in individual departments, provide creativity training, foster non-conformist thinking, and seek to achieve the right composition of their teams by selecting the members carefully from the outset.

If important changes are called for when you take over your new position, you must find out how open to innovation your company or area is. In doing so, however, you should not confine yourself to assessing the current situation. You should instead focus above all on discovering the existing potential.

1. What innovative projects, strategies and changes have been launched recently?

2. Who is responsible for the level of innovation?

3. Are ideas, flexibility and willingness to change nurtured, supported or impeded?

4. Is the emphasis more on goals or on processes?

5. Are there creativity meetings, unconventional task forces, ideas contributed by outsiders, or some combination of these three possibilities?

6. If it is hard to find answers, look for exceptions. They always exist.
   Name important innovative approaches launched in the past two years:

   _____

   _____

   _____

Figure 19 Checklist: how great is the willingness to innovate and change?

SEEK RESOURCES ON WHICH YOU CAN BUILD

If you know the company's rules, understand the culture, identify the issues of concern to the employees, know the facts and can assess the organization's willingness to innovate and change, you still need resources on which to build. In your new position of leadership, you will not be successful if you do not know the strengths of the employees and organization. Whether the strengths lie in the corporate culture, the products, the motivation of the employees, or the strategies, you have to know the strengths on which you can build. This point is especially important if you are swamped with problems and difficulties. In my consulting, I therefore do not get managers to develop their goals before they are able to name the three organizational strengths with which they believe they can be successful.

Bertrand, a young manager at a commercial bank, took over a branch of the organization. He told me that everything had to change. The employees had to work better together; they had to learn to sell and to create new structures. That was the only way to achieve their ambitious goals of increasing turnover with new clients. He pointed out that the branch's business was too dependent on its traditional client base.

I listened patiently to him and asked what he had it in mind to change. My next question was about the resources that would permit him to achieve his objectives. 'Yes, that is a problem. There are not enough, at least nothing that occurs to me directly. On the contrary, the employees are satisfied with the way things are now. They just complain about these new ideas.' I pressed him to think harder and posed another question: 'Assuming that you can meet your goals only if you discover something you can build on, what could that be?'

'Well, reliability', he replied hesitantly and sceptically. 'Is that all? An experienced banking team whose only resource is reliability?' Pressing further, I asked 'Why reliability, anyway? Just when is the staff reliable? There is no art to that, after all.'

Slowly but surely, his attitude changed, and his fixation on the weak points gave way to a cautious look at the staff's strengths. He started to recognize the existing potential.

Such behaviour is quite typical of managers. They are trained to recognize the weak points and to attack the problems head-on. If in addition they are under pressure to succeed, they find it very hard to change gear. In contrast, successful managers have the ability to discover resources. More than that, they help their employees discover the strengths that make it possible to turn the tide. Many employees and departments are in fact utterly unaware of their own strengths.

It is not possible to initiate significant changes without building on existing organizational strengths. The questions in the checklist in Figure 21 will help you to identify the strengths in your people and your organization.

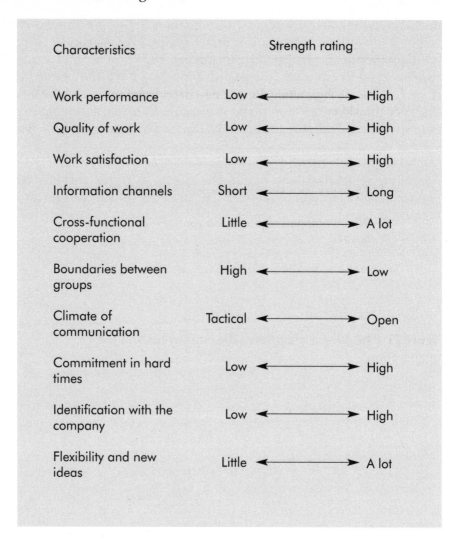

Characteristics	Strength rating		
Work performance	Low	←——————→	High
Quality of work	Low	←——————→	High
Work satisfaction	Low	←——————→	High
Information channels	Short	←——————→	Long
Cross-functional cooperation	Little	←——————→	A lot
Boundaries between groups	High	←——————→	Low
Climate of communication	Tactical	←——————→	Open
Commitment in hard times	Low	←——————→	High
Identification with the company	Low	←——————→	High
Flexibility and new ideas	Little	←——————→	A lot

Figure 20 The strengths of your department

1. Name three strengths your new department can build on:

   _____

   _____

   _____

2. What are your employees especially proud of?

3. What untapped resources do your new employees have?

Figure 21 Checklist: strengths of the employees and the organization

Culture	**1.**	I know the important rules around here, and I understand the corporate culture.
	2.	I know the norms and taboos of the culture and know what will be especially difficult for the employees.
Issues	**3.**	I know the issues of concern to the organization.
	4.	I know how to assess the issues, and the employees also know from my questions how to distinguish what can be solved from what cannot.
	5.	I know the persistent issues and know who has tried to deal with them.
Facts	**6.**	I know the results, the competitive position, market strategies and costs.
	7.	I know with whom my department's employees work together, which interfaces within the company work, and which do not.
	8.	I know the objectives of customers and other departments.
Innovation	**9.**	I know which changes have been made in recent years, which have been successful, and which have not.
	10.	I know the rules and habits that foster innovation and flexibility.
Resources	**11.**	I know the strengths of the employees, the culture and the organization.
	12.	I am convinced that our goals are achievable with these strengths

Figure 22 Summary of Building Block 3

Building Block 4

Establishing a set of motivating goals

'Improve the information flow in the department'

'Foster team spirit'

'Improve the planning for peak business periods'

'Stimulate better cooperation'

'Redistribute responsibilities'

'Introduction to IT'

'Find fairer arrangements for filling in for absent employees'

'Improve cooperation with the IT department'

'Offer systematic staff development'

'Provide training in telephone communication'

Improve the information flow, upgrade IT support, enhance cooperation with the neighbouring department, improve the scheduling of peak stress periods, find fairer arrangements for covering absences, intensify customer orientation, offer systematic staff development – these were just a few of the topics that a newly appointed department head brought to a consulting session with me. Six weeks earlier, he had started a new job in the personnel department, patiently writing down what was expected of him. People had come to him from all sides and had cautiously, but distinctly, named the issues awaiting a solution.

- How do I take the multitude of issues and problems and forge a coherent concept for the change in leadership?
- Which issues do I address, and which do I ignore?
- What criteria should be used to set priorities?
- How do I develop a motivating vision from all these issues?

These questions confront every new manager. Before turning to them, however, let's take a look at what employees in such situations expect from their new boss.

WHAT DO EMPLOYEES LOOK FOR IN A CHANGE OF LEADERSHIP?

If you ask employees what they expect of their new boss, you will hear vastly different answers. The concerns of the employees range from questions about the newcomer's personal style of leadership and way of dealing with criticism to his or her personal weaknesses. They want to know how long the person is staying and what the career path has been so far. They look, albeit not always openly, for information that will enable them to size up the kind of human being their new boss is and what personal interests he or she brings to the new position.

In many workshops with new bosses and their employees, we have learned how important the question about the newcomer's motives is for employees. They want to know whether it will be worth adapting to the new person. For instance, if they find out that he or she has taken on the position for two years or less, they are understandably reticent. They think very carefully about how much to engage and on which issues. The new person needs solid arguments to persuade them to join in on working out new concepts and changes of long-term significance.

Employees also become reticent if they know that their new supervisor has a record of rapid career advancement in recent years. They fear that this person will use them only as a springboard for his or her career and not look after their own long-term needs and interests. Here, too, the new boss must think about how to motivate the employees.

Similar problems are experienced by managers who assume a position abroad. Apart from the employees' scepticism about whether the newcomer is able to acquire an understanding of the cultural differences that exist, they watch closely how well the foreign manager adapts to the new location. In some cases, tension subsides and constructive collaboration commences only after the manager has sent an unmistakable signal of commitment by moving to the new location.

Besides the questions about the new boss's personal motives – enquiries about which the employees expect a straightforward answer – they are interested in what he or she has in mind. In the leadership transition workshops that my team runs, one of the questions repeatedly posed to new bosses is 'Do you already have ideas about how you will approach your new task?'

What lies behind this question is, first, the understandable interest in being informed early about what is going to change. Of course, the initial situation in the department plays a decisive role in this regard. If the results are poor or if the department is the subject of attention for other reasons, the employees usually assume that their new boss is arriving with a number of change targets from top management. But even when the unit has a reputation for having delivered solid work so far, one of the first questions that employees put to their new boss is whether he or she already has a plan and where their ideas will fit into it.

As already pointed out in Building Block 1, you usually have to prepare yourself for a blend of the hope for change and the desire for stability. Unfortunately, one of the biggest mistakes that I encounter

1. How long are you staying?
In other words: Is it worth adapting
to you?

2. What targets have you been given?
In other words: Are you a threat?

3. What do you do in your spare time?
In other words: Are you also human?

4. How have you come to this position?
In other words: What connections or
power do you have?

5. What have you done up to now?
In other words: What experience do you
bring to this assignment?

6. What do you plan to do?
In other words: What is going to change
around here?

Figure 23 What employees want to know about you

again and again consists in creating new structures too quickly. If those changes divest the employees of authority or tasks of which they are especially proud, immediate and substantial resistance is likely. Intended or not, the immediate signal sent to the employees by the rash creation of new structures is that their previous work is evidently little appreciated.

On the other hand, they also want a plan. They want to know where they are going. They want to know what is going to change, where they can lend a helping hand and what impression their new boss has of the team. Moreover, employees whose performance has been unsatisfactory for a while are waiting for a programme that will bring them back up to speed and allow them to feel proud again.

The cornerstones for the development of a programme capable of motivating the employees to strive for ambitious goals are:

- The programme must make clear that the new boss does not intend to impose some preconceived plan on the employees without recognizing the special features of their situation.

- The programme must show the employees that it takes into account both their boss's legitimate interest in success and their own long-term interests.

- The programme must be characterized by a balance between stability and change and must show respect for significant achievements of the team.

- The programme must be easy to communicate tangibly and inspiringly both within the company and to the outside world.

DESIGNING A COMMUNICABLE SET OF GOALS

Management of change is a process of communication. In the section on networking, I stressed that formal authority is seldom enough to initiate important changes. The idea is to formulate a set of goals that the employees find convincing. Most managers initiate changes near the end of the quarter, that is, around the end of the famous 'first 100 days' in the job. By then, they have gathered enough information to have gained a reasonably accurate picture of the situation.

Successful managers are not only able to look at the multitude of issues facing them and choose the 'right' ones. They also cluster them in a way that conveys a persuasive message to the employees. The programmes that these managers develop create a balance between objective necessities and the interest of the employees, between unavoidable changes and necessary stability, and between recognition of past achievements and the call for innovation. Successful leaders also convincingly communicate to the employees that the desired changes are feasible only by building on existing strengths.

Just as sales strategies are conceived today from the customers' point of view, new bosses should develop their strategy of leadership change from the perspective of the employees. That certainly doesn't mean they do what the employees want. On the contrary, that response would be condemned as overt adaptation. But they should examine desired goals for their effects on employees.

Drawing on years of consulting experience with managers in transition, my team and I have designed a simple but extremely effective model to help new leaders devise a motivating set of goals. The model distinguishes between stability-related and change-related goals. Managers today are usually trained to think in terms of goals and goal achievement. They assume it is not necessary to discuss what they feel is obvious and are highly fixated on the changes they have in mind. Such a one-sided set of goals is liable to give employees the impression that their past achievements have been for nothing, especially when they cannot yet size up the newcomer.

For all the changes that may be necessary, say, in sales strategy, a positive climate in a department is particularly valuable. Indeed, it is absolutely essential for successful strategic change and therefore ought to be addressed explicitly. Our experience shows that new managers should always be sure to formulate *at least one stability-related goal for every three goals related to change*. It is the only way to generate a positive climate for change.

In addition to the distinction between goals focused on stability and those focused on change, we have included a dimension intended to help managers avoid another kind of one-sidedness. When we ask managers about their goals, 80 per cent of their responses are task-oriented. This preponderance seems unexceptional and obvious. After all, managers are initially faced with a wide range of issues such as to increase sales, raise profitability or improve quality.

In the eyes of the employees, this common focus on goal setting also harbours a danger. They are liable to gain the impression that the newcomer will concentrate only on tasks. The mood and interaction in the team and the individual employees' personal interests are not reflected in the manager's set of goals. For this reason, we have placed team and personal goals in their own category complementing task-related goals. Improving the work climate, preserving effective cooperation, increasing flexibility and supporting individual employees are all goals that should not be overlooked.

Goals	Stability	Change
Task-related	• Efforts to optimize processes • Independence and personal responsibility	• Introduction of IT • Establishment of process-oriented teams
Team-related	• Space for self-organization	• Fairer arrangements for filling in for absent employees • Regular team meetings
Employee-related		• Formulation of individual development plans • Targeted individual development

Figure 24 Charting objectives: examples

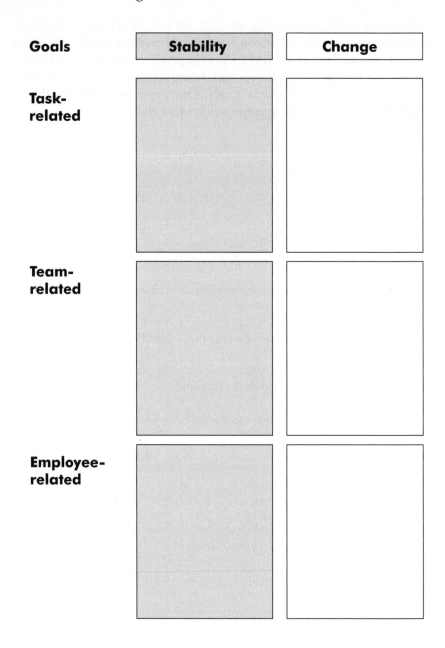

Figure 25 Charting your objectives

When you work out your goals and combine them into a communicable concept, make sure you keep this threefold set of objectives in mind as a model. It should help you produce the most balanced possible set of objectives. Be careful, however, not to overload your future activity with too many goals. Our experience shows that a coherent concept cannot accommodate more than five of them.

1. What goals have you been given?

2. What goals have you already developed for yourself?

3. What goals cannot be dropped under any circumstances?

4. What are your goals for stability?

5. What goals are your pursuing for the team and the individual employees?

6. For which goals do you already have acceptance?

7. Which goals can you pursue at a later time?

8. If you have to confine yourself to three, four or five goals, which would you choose?

9. What goals can you cluster into a communicable vision?

Figure 26 Checklist: identify goals for your new department

AVOIDING THE PITFALLS WHEN FORMULATING GOALS

Better results, lower costs, a better climate and more initiative are typical goals challenging managers today. If such goals are to be met, they have to be spelled out. There is more to such general formulations than first meets the eye. You discover what lies behind them when you start asking questions like: What does 'better' mean? Why better? Who judges better, and what criteria are there by which to judge the improvement?

Mistake 1: Working with general goals

For example, 'customer orientation' means not only putting yourself in the customer's shoes but also ensuring constant feedback on the effect of your measures and much more. Upon close inspection, the often obvious goal of improving cooperation within the team quickly becomes a major demand too. What would better cooperation actually look like? What has thwarted it thus far? What would be the first step towards achieving this goal?

These questions are a few of those requiring an answer if a solution is to be found. The general goals have to be dissected into their component parts before you can realistically assess the effort it will mean to make it part of your strategy.

Again and again, a typical problem of leadership transition is the hasty formulation of subsequently unachievable goals. Managers are trapped into taking action precipitately under the presumed pressure of charting a course quickly. The result is a loss of credibility.

Positive–negative

Negative goals such as 'fewer conflicts' tend to come to mind first. They are not helpful, for they do not say what is supposed to be done.

Central–peripheral

Far too many peripheral problems are addressed only because they appear to be pressing. Central problems are recognizable by their effect on the system at large.

General–specific

The goal of creating 'a better climate' is not a helpful goal either. It is far too general and thus does not enable you to assess the chances of meeting it.

Implicit–explicit

If you want to achieve a particular goal, such as improving relations with the neighbouring department, then a number of related, implicit goals quickly arise. More solidarity in important strategic decisions and making your department stand out may be implicit goals that are liable to be forgotten.

Figure 27 Some typical mistakes in formulating goals

Mistake 2: Working on urgent problems rather than on the really important ones

If you manage to derive precise goals from the general ones, be careful to avoid a second mistake. New managers all too often fail to assess the significance of the goals correctly. They attack the problems that are presented to them as being urgent, and there are plenty of those associated with every change in leadership. Everyone is waiting for the newcomer to solve, at last, all the long-standing problems.

The incorrect assessment of the size of the problems being approached, especially at the beginning, often has to do with the fact that the general goals were not carefully and completely broken down into their component parts. The German psychologist Dörner calls this pattern 'maintenance behaviour'. He has repeatedly

> When Renata assumed her new position as production manager, she received a long list of issues from her boss. Everyone had been waiting for some time for a solution, as the position had been filled by an interim manager for six months. After familiarizing herself with the job for a relatively short time, Renata began to work on seeing to the quick and reliable provision of the sales information necessary for guiding production. She ignored the initial scepticism and warnings of some of the employees, interpreting them as exaggerated pessimism. Not until two or three months later did she realize that other bright people had tried the same thing before her and that the task was by no means as simple to master as she had originally thought.

observed it in his studies, even among seasoned managers. Having recognized two important issues, some of the participants in the studies evidently could not wait to begin seeking a solution although they had not yet clarified the size and significance of the problem.

Mistake 3: Considering the goals in isolation

A third mistake you should avoid is that of considering each goal in isolation. You will find it helpful to write all the problems down in a long list and think about how they relate to one another. You will quickly find that some goals grow out of others. For instance, the results of a sales team are the outcome not only of the performance of the individual employees on site but of many additional variables as well. Furthermore, by comparing goals on your list, you will see that some of them are actually rather marginal or less critical than others.

Sales strategies, communication between internal and field services, the positioning of individual employees, and motivation are no less important. In principle, they are points of departure for a new sales director if he or she wants to affect the result.

However, you must consider the potential significance of different factors in the new situation.

> When Martin took over a team of seven people in Eastern Europe, he suspected from their suboptimal training that they were not assigned to the right jobs. In one of the first meetings of the team, Martin and his people discussed what criteria would help them determine which tasks should be assigned to which person. The discussion automatically led to a change in internal communication about success and strategies, which ultimately affected performance.

Linear thinking is a trap in these situations. What you need is a systemic approach that allows you to see connections between different parts of the picture. Results, market developments and problems in the company are always the outcome of many interconnected variables. In such situations, it is not a matter of throwing as many resources as possible at a problem. Instead, what you need to do is to focus the resources you have in the most effective way on the situation at hand. In order to do that, you need to visualize how the important variables interact.

VISIONS – LOOKING TO THE FUTURE

As management professor Hermann Simon has stated, 'Only the person with visions can use strategic resources purposefully.' For visions not only show the way but generate their own power by offering employees the possibility of identification.

Vision is a great and, especially in recent years, overworked word. One almost automatically thinks of the visions of the founders of major companies, such as Robert Bosch, Gottfried Daimler or Henry Ford.

But do not be put off by this thought. We are not talking about the development of your life's work but rather about a courageous look into the future. In fact, visionary thinking just means keeping your thinking from being determined solely by current problems. It means focusing on the goal you are working toward. *In other words, someone with a vision first describes the goal, not the way to it.*

Effective leaders paint a picture of the desired future state, as is illustrated in the following description: 'I imagine us having an excellent position in the market in two to three years. We have improved our market share by 10 per cent. We meet with our important customers, and we develop new concepts at our team off-site retreats. We meet regularly and feel jointly responsible for success.' When this new manager spoke to the members of his team, he not only mapped out an indisputably ambitious result but also described the interaction within the team. These images help give the employees an idea of where they are headed on their journey. As advised by the wise author of *The Little Prince* and *The Wisdom of the Sands*, Antoine de Saint-Exupéry, 'If you want to build a ship, don't drum up people to collect wood and don't assign them tasks and work, but rather teach them to long for the endless immensity of the sea.' In this spirit, ask yourself the questions in the checklist in Figure 28.

1. What goals do you want to have achieved two years from now?

2. What will be this department's striking characteristics two years from now?

3. How will the employees interact with each other?

4. What will your interaction with other departments be like?

5. What will you be satisfied with and which new challenges will you address?

Figure 28 Checklist: questions to stimulate visionary thinking

1. Employees want a concept that will take them forward and fill them with pride.

2. Your employees are like customers. Design a set of customer-centred goals.

3. Maintain a balance between stability and change.

4. Paint a picture of the future.

Some typical mistakes to avoid:

- attacking the problems that urgently need to be solved;

- calling for quick changes by pointing out the problems;

- tackling things before you gain a picture of the overall situation.

Figure 29 Summary of Building Block 4

Building Block 5

Fostering a positive climate for change

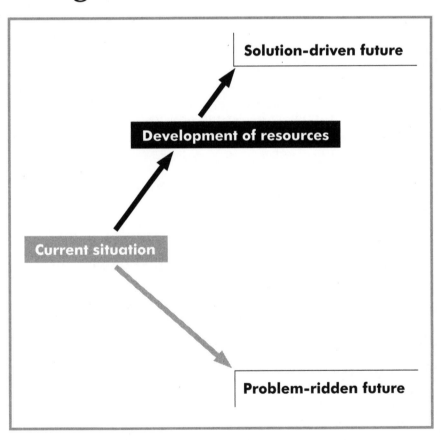

One decisive thing that successful managers are able to achieve from the outset is a positive climate for change. How do they do that? How do they emotionally attune the employees to the changes under consideration, and how do they overcome the scepticism that almost always exists? How do they manage even to develop the desire for something new and thereby pave the way for ambitious projects?

Three things appear to be vital in this process:

1. *Ask an appreciative question, get an appreciative response.* Managers who are successful at making transitions in leadership are not only highly communicative. They are also able to ask appreciative questions that give the employees a feeling of strength and a glimpse of the future.

2. *Deal positively with scepticism.* Managers who are successful at making transitions in leadership also evidently have the ability to deal with employee scepticism so skilfully that they are not stymied by it.

3. *Instil a desire for something new.* Managers who are successful at making transitions in leadership are curious. They are discoverers who create a culture that fosters a positive attitude toward innovation and change.

Now let us consider each of these three skills of successful managers.

ASK AN APPRECIATIVE QUESTION, GET AN APPRECIATIVE RESPONSE

It is necessary to look very closely to discover where successful new leaders differ from less successful ones. An important factor is that managers who are successful at making transitions in leadership ask questions differently. They do *not* ask about problems, especially in the early stages. When they gather information by talking to their employees – and they do so consistently and thoroughly – they prompt them to describe precisely how everything works. They ask about the processes and the interaction between the departments. They ask about the important differences between departments and important changes in the past. They ask about the problems that have been solved and the strengths that were necessary for those tasks. They ask about important achievements and pending changes. Question by question, with great respect for what was done in the past, they systematically piece together a picture of the initial situation.

These are called 'reflective questions' because they get people to think. Such questions are powerful because they serve not only for gathering information but also for creating new information.

Reflective questions

- 'What is the difference between department A and department B?'
- 'How do you explain department B's lack of support?'
- 'What would be the consequences for your department if nothing changed?'
- 'What other explanations could department B have for its lack of support?'

Resourceful questions

- 'What products are the employees in your department especially proud of?'
- 'How did you manage to get through last year despite the tight personnel situation?'
- 'What strengths do you typically have in hard times?'

Future-oriented questions

- 'What issues will occupy us two years from now?'
- 'How will you know that you have reached your goal?'
- 'What surprises will we encounter?'

Figure 30 Ask an appreciative question, get an appreciative answer

I get the desired information to begin with if I do not simply ask the employees where the problems are but rather request them to explain the difference between departments A and B to me. In addition, such questions prompt the person I am speaking with to reflect further on that difference. By then asking how he or she would explain department B's lack of support and whether there are other explanations, I show that I want to get a feeling for different views. Slowly but surely, I thereby develop a climate in which existing views can be challenged and new views can be formed.

Successful managers in new positions use a second group of questions as well. These are called 'resourceful questions', meaning questions intended to help systematically identify strengths. Changes require trust in one's own strengths. But people are often not aware of their strengths, so the new manager's role is to cultivate this awareness. Therefore, ask your employees about the departmental projects they are proud of, how they managed to get through last year despite the tight personnel situation, what strengths they have honed in the last two years, what strengths they used to have, and what would be needed to regain them.

What you should not do under any circumstances if you are interested in establishing a positive climate for change is ask about the cause of problems. Apart from the fact that you will seldom receive constructive answers, the question will only lead to unnecessary justifications. It is considerably more helpful to assume that the employees have so far undertaken everything they could to solve the problems at hand.

This hypothesis regularly triggers intense discussions in seminars. It seems to contradict experience, and many managers find it hard to take such a perspective. But it is the only sensible working hypothesis. It is the basic attitude necessary for ensuring that your employees actually begin to discover their strengths.

DEAL POSITIVELY WITH SCEPTICISM

No matter how appreciative your interview strategies are, in many instances you will encounter a sizeable degree of scepticism among the employees. If you are, say, the third person in three years to try setting up a particular kind of service important to the company, then the ability to deal with scepticism becomes a key competence.

Employees may not believe there can be a solution to their problems. Perhaps for the last three years they have been struggling with the telephone system, which has kept creating new obstacles. As a result, they have been hearing customers' complaints about excessively long delays and they have been complaining about completely inadequate production information. They may already have attempted technical solutions many times and made untold efforts to communicate, yet achieved no breakthrough. The mood will be correspondingly negative. Not surprisingly, the new manager will encounter doubt, even though he or she is obviously competent. Announcing a strategy for success, as a predecessor had, would only reinforce the scepticism.

What is important in such situations? What should the newcomer do to succeed?

- *Meet the scepticism positively.* Welcome scepticism. It protects against exaggerated expectations and often contains a number of clues to possible obstacles that are liable to be overlooked. It also shows that the employees are interested in the issue. Otherwise, they would not express anything at all. One of the most frequent mistakes in dealing with sceptical employees is to put their concerns down immediately as 'destructive' behaviour. Lurking behind such a response is the concern that this attitude will infect others, possibly even the new boss. Managers quickly feel threatened by scepticism and try to get rid of it fast. By doing so, however, they not only put themselves at odds with the employees right from the start but also run the risk of becoming caught in a vicious circle.

- *Differentiate the scepticism.* When my team and I encounter scepticism in our workshops with employees and their new leaders, we ask the employees to write down on a card all the points that could block the successful implementation of the proposed strategy. The result is always very interesting:

  - Stated and unstated scepticism are not the same thing. When people have to formulate their scepticism, many different points emerge. It quickly turns out that some employees are sceptical about the logic of the strategy, whereas others doubt whether it can be implemented. Still others are sceptical that it will be followed consistently. If we probe further, asking

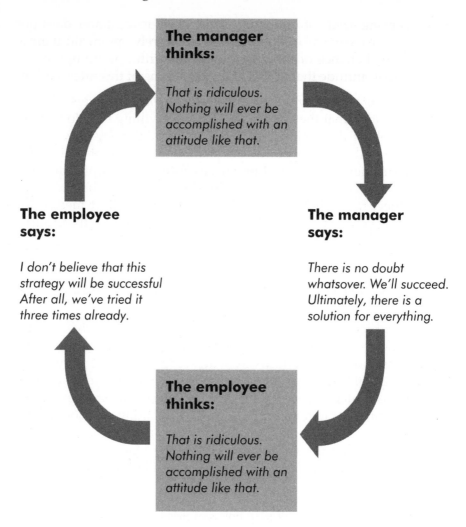

The manager thinks:

That is ridiculous. Nothing will ever be accomplished with an attitude like that.

The employee says:

I don't believe that this strategy will be successful After all, we've tried it three times already.

The manager says:

There is no doubt whatsover. We'll succeed. Ultimately, there is a solution for everything.

The employee thinks:

That is ridiculous. Nothing will ever be accomplished with an attitude like that.

Figure 31 Optimists and pessimists: a vicious circle that nobody wants

which aspect is the most stubborn obstacle to the successful pursuit of a strategy, then the initial, apparently massive, scepticism becomes increasingly differentiated.

– When the scepticism is made visible to everyone in the room, a second effect occurs. The group almost always starts reacting against so much scepticism and in fact begins experiencing seeds of optimism. If the boss or facilitator does not make the mistake of becoming prematurely optimistic, there is a real chance of infusing the group with a more optimistic basic attitude than it had at the beginning of this intervention.

● *Beware of coming across as an optimistic prophet.* Managers who are persuaded that there is a solution to everything tend to take on the role of the optimist all too soon. They thereby unwittingly deprive the employees of the chance to surmount their scepticism themselves. Dealing successfully with scepticism thus means keeping your own basic positive attitude in balance with respect for well-founded scepticism. Above all, it means not letting yourself get positioned as the sole optimist in the group.

CLIMATE – THE BASIS OF ALL CHANGE

The initial requirements for the development of a positive climate for change – eliciting appreciative responses through appreciative questions and dealing effectively with scepticism – determine early in a change of leadership whether a constructive climate for change can be generated. Every experienced manager knows that all the sound arguments in favour of the changes awaiting decision will be of little use if the requisite climate does not exist among the employees. What does a positive climate for change mean? What variables are characteristic of it and how can it be affected?

Maria took over a team of six employees in the sales department of a major office machine manufacturer. The employees sold the equipment, serviced it and maintained customer contact. Even before Maria assumed the position, she had been told that the assignment would be a difficult one. The employees were allegedly very diverse and poorly motivated, and they were said to have little contact with other groups. Maria was told that her predecessor had considerable trouble leading the group in the previous year and had sought a different position for that reason. Maria also heard that important structural changes were in the offing and that the team in its current condition would probably have little chance of coping with them.

Maria encountered a destructive mood right from the first meeting of the team. Because she had been forewarned, she did not let it affect her. She saw that she was not dealing with a functioning team but rather was facing six individuals who had little to do with each other. They complained about their lack of information, the personnel shortage, the poor sales strategy and the situation of their own team. They knew that Maria came from a team regarded as highly successful and harmonious. During a break, each one of them inquired about her experience. However, they also showed themselves to be very sceptical about whether it was transferable.

Maria announced she had heard that these six people had gone through quite a hard time. She explained that she therefore wanted to take the time in the next three to four weeks to speak to each of them individually. She would seek them out, visit customers with them and meet with them afterwards.

These discussions were the beginning of a change in the climate. In long personal conversations, Maria learned about their experience, desires, missed development and much more. She spoke with them about their collaboration in the team and about opportunities to foster it.

At the second team meeting, which Maria set up carefully, she asked them to report in detail about their customers, not only those they had successfully worked with so far but also those with whom they had experienced problems. She thereby opened a strategy discussion of a kind that had not existed for a long time in the team. Because Maria had never sought to discuss possible changes but rather had focused solely on the potential that had become apparent in the group, this team off-site meeting passed in a very relaxed manner. She took advantage of this positive experience to ask one of the employees to set up the next team meeting. She stressed that this approach represented an important principle for her because the members of the team were ultimately the ones who could judge best how the away-day should be handled so that they all benefited from it.

After a solid half-year of intensive work with the individual employees, numerous carefully prepared team conferences, and the skilful assignment of tasks, Maria finally succeeded in creating a climate that was ready for quite significant structural changes. The employees had regained confidence in their abilities and had learned to share information with each other. Maria could therefore begin to discuss new sales strategies and start a regional redistribution of sales responsibilities.

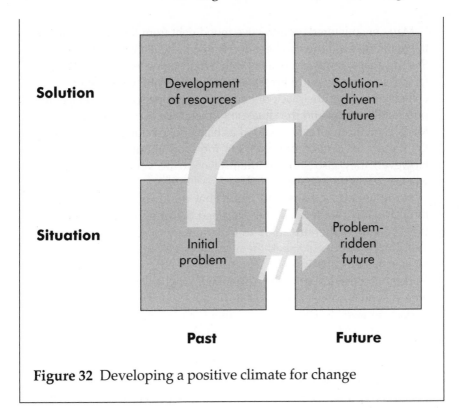

Figure 32 Developing a positive climate for change

The image of the heroic new boss who acts quickly and assertively still exists in many companies. These leadership strategies seldom work. In some cases when the corporate situation is extremely difficult and little time is left to make the necessary changes, there is no other choice. In most cases, however, the newcomer is well advised to plough the ground before sowing. Considerably less energy is wasted in the process, and the returns are much greater. Therefore, you will find it helpful to ask yourself the questions in the checklist in Figure 33.

1. How much trust do the employees have in my abilities?

2. What do I know about their strengths?

3. What strengths urgently have to be developed?

4. What projects can develop the strengths?

Figure 33 Checklist: introduce changes carefully

1. Start by developing a positive climate for change. It is one of the first tasks in leadership transitions.

2. Treat your employees with respect and show appreciation of their achievements, especially when they do not believe in themselves.

3. Show recognition through questions and foster the willingness to adopt other points of view.

4. Welcome expressions of scepticism. They contain valuable clues to possible obstacles.

5. Beware of assuming the role of the optimist. It invariably keeps the others in the role of the pessimist.

Some typical mistakes to avoid:

- zeroing in only on problems right from the beginning;
- focusing on the weaknesses of your employees;
- believing that only your optimism can help in this situation;
- fighting uphill battles against negative moods.

Figure 34 Summary of Building Block 5

Building Block 6

Initiating changes effectively

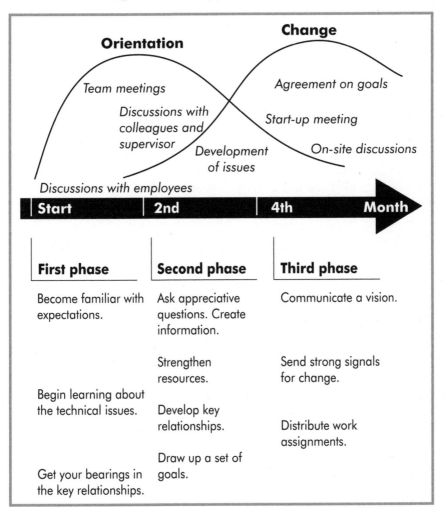

Orientation

Change

Team meetings

Agreement on goals

Discussions with colleagues and supervisor

Start-up meeting

On-site discussions

Development of issues

Discussions with employees

| Start | 2nd | 4th | Month |

First phase	**Second phase**	**Third phase**
Become familiar with expectations.	Ask appreciative questions. Create information.	Communicate a vision.
	Strengthen resources.	Send strong signals for change.
Begin learning about the technical issues.	Develop key relationships.	Distribute work assignments.
Get your bearings in the key relationships.	Draw up a set of goals.	

Assuming that you now know what people expect, have developed important key relationships, have drawn up a set of goals and have prepared the employees for the pending changes through a number of discussions, the next thing is to deal with the following questions:

- How do I effectively set the changes in motion?

- How do I reach as many of the employees as quickly as possible and thereby implement the new strategy systematically?

- How do I proceed step by step and what obstacles will I encounter?

STRONG SIGNALS FOR CHANGE

Robert took over as head of sales four months ago. In his new position, he is responsible for 80 employees in the field in four regions. In his discussions with the employees and his managers, he pieced together a picture of the initial situation. He has spoken to customers and learned about their situation. His set of goals has crystallized in his mind with ever greater clarity in recent weeks:

- To sharpen the focus on the important target groups.

- To change the management style by delegating responsibility more consistently than in the past.

- To give the employees in the field a new understanding of their role through new sales concepts.

Robert was intent on introducing these goals effectively. He wanted to send a strong signal for change and launch a programme of measures, for time was short. He therefore invited all the employees to an off-site meeting. The date was announced four weeks in advance. The cursory information about the goal of the meeting was 'sales goals'. Of course, this announcement piqued curiosity and fostered an immense number of rumours. But Robert had prepared well. In his many discussions with the employees, he had succeeded in getting not only answers to his questions but also possible ideas for the future. Even more important, his straight-forward, frank manner had enabled him to create so much trust that the employees were looking forward to their off-site meeting with excitement and optimism.

It was to take place in a hotel, beginning at 8 pm. The new director was nowhere to be seen. All the employees were ushered into the large auditorium by the hotel personnel. At the appointed hour, a magician opened the conference. He welcomed the guests and engagingly demonstrated how 'wondrous effects can be achieved by simple means'.

The audience enthusiastically applauded the half-hour presentation, after which the new boss appeared on the stage and introduced his key message: 'Although we are not talking about magic, we are talking about an effect that is almost the same. When it comes to rousing the curiosity of our customers in our sales pitches, we do not need much either.'

Robert then explained what he wanted to focus on for the next year, and a carefully planned sequence of reports, discussions and suggestions followed. Experts had come to present detailed, persuasive concepts and steps relating to each of the goals. The conference ended with a roundtable discussion with a few customers in order to hear their assessments and questions.

Initiating changes effectively means sending strong, clear signals for change. In signalling change, it is important to communicate at an objective as well as an *emotional* level, especially when time is of the essence. Employees must sense that matters are being taken seriously and they need an indication of the many changes that will occur. Whether it is a matter of inaugurating a new sales strategy, instilling a new corporate identity or changing leadership style, it is always worth exploring how you can make the beginning as intense an experience as possible.

Remember, however, that the first action steps need to be taken immediately after the strong signals for change are communicated. Otherwise, this experience will quickly fizzle out or degenerate into a one-off event like so many others.

1. Changes need strong signals. You must not only persuade the employees with sound arguments but also address them at an emotional level.

2. Strong signals for change need a guiding theme that fits the strategy. The theme can focus on:

- what the employees must do;
- what the customers get out of it;
- what the future looks like; and
- what changes are becoming apparent.

3. Strong signals for change must be immediately followed by specific measures. Otherwise, they fade without effect.

Figure 35 Sending strong signals for change

IF I WANT TO CHANGE SOMETHING, I MUST DO SOMETHING DIFFERENT

One of the most frequent mistakes in managing change is not following through resolutely. Such mistakes tend to occur when too little attention has been paid to the change process. In the belief that 'what works for our competitors has to work for us too', some managers announce goals such as an increase in personal responsibility or customer focus without having a clear awareness of what these aspirations involve.

Most changes required in organizations today entail significant shifts in employee attitudes and habits, many of which are hard to change because they are firmly entrenched. To prepare people for change, the initial situation must first be explored carefully. The new manager must not only identify possible hurdles but also find the critical point at which all people concerned can feel that something different is expected of them. In many cases, people have to trip over old habits in order to recognize that they need to behave differently. For instance, if you want to keep your employees from incessantly coming to you with every minor decision, then stop making decisions for your employees in your office.

Upon taking charge, one new plant director felt it was important for his managers to assume more personal responsibility than they had under his predecessor. He explained to the employees that he would be available for consultation on difficult decisions at any time, but not in his office any more. Every employee could in future 'call him over' if it seemed necessary.

This arrangement changed the situation in just a short time. The employees knew what a huge number of issues were occupying their new boss, so they thought twice about whether they should really ask him to come to them. The number of times people tried to delegate decisions to him immediately declined by almost half.

Such an approach to making the desired change apparent in a change of daily habits works in other situations as well. If you want employees to talk to each other, put them together. If you want an employee to work better with another department, give her a project from that department. She is sure to have good ideas and will automatically be compelled to grapple with the expectations and goals of the other department.

To pave the way, however, you must first have succeeded at persuading your employees of the necessity and feasibility of your goals. Otherwise, any changes you introduce will be experienced only as annoying and will remain ineffectual. As Professor Michael Beer, a US organizational consultant, points out, the departure point of any effective measure for change must be a jointly recognized problem in the organization.

However, there are a number of other guidelines you should note if you want to set successful change processes in motion. Nearly all of them rest on the insight that organizational change does not come

Step	Goal	Methods
1.	Joint diagnosis of the initial situation	• Discussions • Workshops
2.	Strong signals for change	• Start-up meeting
3.	Implementation	• Focus on two to three main points • Agreement on goals and first steps
4.	Development of trust in the change process	• Formation of a steering group to establish responsibility • Creation of internal communication on the status of change
5.	Self-monitoring via feedback	• Establishment of feedback loops • Monitoring of progress and corrections

Figure 36 Five steps in managing change

about through application of simplistic rules derived from a mechanistic understanding of the company. The classic logic of planning, announcing and then implementing changes may look good on paper, but it has little to do with reality in organizations, which is essentially a matter of human interaction.

Managing change is a process that must take the complex interplay of people, rules and external influences on companies into account. Once common goals and a shared view of things have been developed, follow through on each change project systematically. Make sure you limit yourself to a manageable number of projects. This approach is a strategy of small wins and large gains, which is designed to begin with issues that permit rapid success and thereby generate the momentum needed for making bigger changes happen.

A consistent 'Good morning, you are speaking to...' instead of the customary 'What do you want...?' leads to the goal of customer orientation faster than long lectures on the importance of customers. At a commercial bank in which this small change was implemented, the employees eventually engaged in a broad discussion about service and changes in a way that had not seemed conceivable before.

The strategy of small wins and large gains has another positive effect. It quickly generates trust in the change process because rapid success is achievable. Managers who are successful in leadership transition also ensure that their employees see change as a continuous process. Their message to sceptics is that 'Once the process has started, it is unstoppable.' Unlike the customary and naive claim that 'Anything is possible', this approach makes it possible to deal with obstacles. The only thing that is beyond doubt is the conviction that 'The goals set will be achieved with the available resources.'

The fifth and final step in managing change is feedback loops. They are necessary to set the required self-monitoring processes in motion. A department that wants to improve teamwork should begin early to create specific kinds of feedback criteria. Employees could check, for example, when and to what degree the team effectively develops and implements solutions to problems. Only in this way is it possible to make the adaptations that are necessary to achieve the intended goal.

TIMING IN LEADERSHIP TRANSITION

One of the most frequently asked questions in our seminars and consulting is when changes should start. Some people quickly put themselves under time pressure; others hesitate because they have the impression that they do not know enough. Without realizing it, they are only inflating expectations.

Identifying the right point in time to initiate change is a key skill in handling a change in leadership successfully. First, you need to be sure that the organization is ready to undertake change. You should begin with change projects if:

- discussions and meetings with you have prepared the employees for change;

- important key relationships that you need for a successful change process have at least begun to develop; and

- a clear concept exists for the first steps.

Our experience has shown that this stage is reached after two to four months, depending on the magnitude of the task and the changes that are being considered. The outsider usually needs somewhat longer – more because the newcomer first needs to build the necessary network of relationships than because he or she is slow in acquiring the needed knowledge. The most impetuous new bosses are the insiders who appear with ready-made concepts and easily forget that they first have to communicate their level of knowledge.

Time is then the second criterion. It is definitely necessary to keep in mind that leadership transitions have a window of opportunity for change, a period during which the employees even expect it. The proverbial '100 days' are a widely known image that is an expression of a widely shared expectation: employees want to know what is going to change. If you, as a new boss, exceed this time frame without apparent reason, you must be aware that the delay will entail a number of disadvantages:

- *Expectations rise.* Your employees start thinking 'If it is taking so long for us to find out where things are headed, then it must be something really special.'

Making changes too early	**Making changes too late**
• You know too little about the organization, its issues and its rules.	• You unavoidably raise expectations and then must deal with reduced tolerance for difficulties.
• You cannot distinguish well enough between what is important and what is not.	• You lose momentum.
• You know too little about where and how policy is made in the company.	• You increasingly lose the newcomer's licence to enquire into habits.
• Your network of relationships is not great enough for you to implement your changes.	• You lose your own distance and become less bold.

Figure 37 Timing risks in leadership transition

- *You lose momentum.* The positive tension of expectations does not last for ever. After three or four months, employees generally relax and sit back.

- *You increasingly lose the newcomer's licence to challenge habits and traditions.* The longer you are around, the more you become associated with the existing state of affairs. The employees understand less and less why you are suddenly calling into question their routine ways of seeing and doing things.

- *You tend to become a part of the system yourself and lose your objective distance.* Changing things generally means challenging established patterns of behaviour. The more reasons you know for 'doing things the way we have always done them around here', the less drive you have for tackling this change.

But timing also demands paying attention to the order of the individual steps. You must decide how much you can and want to take on all at once. The limited resource here is the available management capacity. My team and I repeatedly find that people introduce too many good ideas at the same time without realizing that they must also be implemented.

Your ability to pursue different projects simultaneously and consistently is limited, and so is that of your employees. A simple matrix that you can fill out with your team will help you prevent your positive beginnings from failing out of sheer strain. Just note down in the far left-hand column all the measures you are considering and record in the relevant columns to the right who is going to be affected by them. If you and possibly your team use this matrix for step-by-step, joint planning of who initiates, pursues, observes and implements each activity, then you will quickly have an overview of the overall workload.

SOME OBSTACLES TO THE MANAGEMENT OF CHANGE

One thing is certain: no change process runs without encountering obstacles. Lengthy delays in the change process can ensue from employee scepticism about the likely success of the chosen strategy, from unexpected slumps in earnings and from tedious coordination with internal negotiating partners who suddenly surface.

The art of managers who are successful at leadership transition lies in keeping the change process going despite all the obstacles. This requires you to communicate systematically about each indicator of progress in the change and to deal constructively with obstacles.

Measures	Top management	Area management	Department head	Department	Team	Customer
1.						
2.						
3.						
4.						
5.						

Tasks: Show direction • Initiate • Shape • Apply • Implement • Work
Responsibility: Mark an 'x' in the column where responsibility for each activity lies.

Figure 38 Measures and their effects: an implementation matrix

Most problems in the management of change, however, are of your own making:

- Starting without sufficient preparation is one of the most frequent mistakes. There are still many managers who believe that management consists in the intellectual task of designing a coherent concept. Actually, *management is first and foremost about communication*, especially when it comes to changes in leadership. The employees want to be well prepared for the pending change (see Building Block 5 for details).

- The second most common mistake made in the management of change is the formulation of vague goals. More customer orientation, a higher degree of flexibility and a positive attitude toward innovation may all be great slogans, but they are no help for specific changes.

- The third mistake is the adoption of an unrealistic time line for change. Many managers still underestimate the time that some changes require. For example, it is reasonable to expect the introduction of a new approach to customer management to take a whole year. The 'development of more team spirit', another common goal, will take about the same amount of time. In fact, one seasoned manager who had made several successful leadership transitions cautioned that, in his experience, restructuring would take the organization about two years to digest. In all my years of consulting, this executive was the only one who applied such a realistic time frame.

- The fourth mistake has already come up in various ways. Change managers who experience obstacles as disruptions or annoyances rather than as stimuli or indications of possible risks create unnecessary problems for themselves.

- The fifth crucial mistake made in the course of managing change is inadequate communication. Often, only results are reported, a practice that leaves too much time and space for unconstructive rumours to circulate in the intervals between reports.

1. Are the employees prepared for the changes?   Yes   No
   What else do I need to do?

2. Have we identified problems together?   Yes   No
   What else do I need to do?

3. Which time frame am I in from the employees' point of view?
   Too early _____   On time _____   Too late _____

4. Which key message can I use to send strong signals for initiating change?

5. Who must I include in the process of initiating change?
   1. _____   5. _____
   2. _____   6. _____
   3. _____   7. _____
   4. _____   8. _____

6. Do I know what needs to be done immediately
   after the signal for change is given?   Yes   No
   What else do I need to do?

7. Is the existing management capacity adequate?   Yes   No
   What can I postpone?

8. Who will be responsible for each part of the change process?
   Measure 1: _____
   Measure 2: _____
   Measure 3: _____

9. How do I ensure feedback on the change process and its outcomes?
   1. _____
   2. _____
   3. _____

10. When is the continual process of change scheluded to begin?
    Step 1: _____
    Step 2: _____

Figure 39 Checklist: initiate change effectively

1. The point of departure for change must be a jointly recognized problem.

2. The organization needs to be prepared for change.

3. Bear in mind the strategy of 'small wins and large gains'.

4. Approach the change from several strategic angles.

5. Check that you have the necessary management capacity.

6. Ensure that continual progress is made.

Some typical mistakes to avoid:

- shooting from the hip;
- beginning too many things at once;
- insisting on planning and controlling everything;
- fighting obstacles.

Figure 40 Summary of Building Block 6

Building Block 7

Using symbols and rituals

Max had taken over as CEO two weeks previously. His predecessor had been at the helm of the corporation for 10 years, and the company had been very successful under his leadership. Max thought highly of him. When Max had been the director of an important foreign subsidiary, the two men had worked together well, although they were very different. This predecessor was a rather reserved, visionary man who loved art. His far-sightedness had led the corporation into new fields of business. Max, by contrast, was extroverted and liked to have his finger on the pulse of business, and he had an indomitable will to act on things. In the previous three years, he had led the foreign subsidiary through difficult structural change and had brought it on to a path convergent with that of the corporation.

Max began unobtrusively. He first moved into his predecessor's office without changing much. He sought out many people for discussions and learned how top management meetings had been run in the organization. He asked why each item on the agenda was placed where it was rather than at some other place and why there were so many one-to-one discussions.

One morning in his fourth week – he had meanwhile been at a number of external meetings, and the employees were already beginning to ask themselves what he was likely to change – he entered the office and asked two members of his staff to walk around the place with him. He quietly gazed at the pictures in the corridor and the meeting rooms and thought about changes with his colleagues; then he gave instructions on how pictures and furniture needed to be moved. The meeting room occupied him most. He knew that it would be the most important place for decision making, but the table was too long for effective top-management team meetings. He realized that the challenges lying ahead and the structural changes needed to meet them would require much more teamwork than his predecessor had used. He therefore decided to change the layout and furnishings of his own office, where he intended to hold most meetings. The furniture was to be friendly, straightforward and not too expensive. Most significantly, he asked that a new table be brought into his office to replace the sitting-corner arrangement his predecessor had used for his one-to-one conversations.

Symbolic language is powerful. All of the world's successful managers have mastered it. They use the opportunity to add weight with symbols and rituals. They pay attention to the design of their meetings, establish rituals to support employee identification with the company, and honour the successes of top sales reps at special annual celebrations. Similarly, assessment centres are not just a means of professionalizing human resource decisions. The practice of running assessment centres and bringing in external corporate consultants has a strong symbolic meaning that the typical rituals underscore.

THE SIGNIFICANCE OF SYMBOLS AND RITUALS IN THE PROCESS OF LEADERSHIP TRANSITION

During a change in leadership, an important part of the new manager's challenge is to establish contact with a large number of employees in a relatively short period of time. This situation is precisely where it makes sense to use the language of symbols and rituals.

The first key message in such a transition is about the presence of the new leader. If you review Max's story, you will find how skilfully staged it is in this regard. The initial reserve demonstrated by the new CEO was necessary. A predecessor who has led the organization successfully for a long time cannot immediately be 'erased'. That person must 'linger in the rooms' for a while in order to allow the employees time to bid him or her farewell and adapt to the new leader.

After showing deference to the predecessor's symbols and rituals, however, the important thing is to make your own presence unmistakably clear. As is always the case with strong personalities, the point is to mark the beginning of a new, different era. This message can be conveyed with words, of course, but better yet is to emphasize it with signs. Max's instructions on how to alter the furniture and decor sent strong signals for change to his employees. Similarly, the fact that he chose to do this by walking and talking with members of his staff indicated the future style of leadership.

My team and I have seen what happens when insensitive managers disregard the symbolic aspect of their actions. In a particularly painful case, a foreign corporation took over a family business employing 1,000 people that had been led for 20 years by the founders. After only a few days, the new managers changed the offices, the structure of the meetings, the reporting practices and much more. To them, it seemed a practical necessity to bring the company quickly into their corporation. To their surprise, the new acquisition very soon lost three of its most important managers. Having found the actions 'indicative of the new company', they had decided not to stick around any longer. By unwittingly confirming the fear among many of the employees that the new owners would show little respect for their time-tested structures, the incoming managers had immediately and unnecessarily stoked a great deal of scepticism and resistance.

Clearly, considering symbols and rituals in isolation sheds little light on their power. Popular management books that highlight and describe individual elements are misleading. They give the impression that all a manager needs to do is put up a couple of bulletin boards in the room and, hey presto, a symbol for a new leadership style has been found.

Symbolic management is the skilful and consistent combination of symbols and rituals into a convincing message. A frequent problem is that many managers have learned far too little about examining their own actions for the implicit messages they send. A new human resource director wondered why the response had been so low-key to the message he had announced just a few weeks after assuming his position. He had advocated that 'We must develop the next generation', unaware that this message was bound to raise concerns simply because he spoke too early. The employees could not yet size him up, so a large number of older ones wondered whether they had any future in the company.

Behaviour always has two components: an 'objective' (or 'technical') aspect and a 'symbolic' dimension. For instance, making changes in agendas is usually seen as a 'technical', or practical, act. But in a process of leadership transition it always also conveys a message about the intentions of the newcomer. This is why it is important to ensure that what you say is consistent with how you behave. When the new boss breaks with the customary procedure by regularly starting team meetings with a report on customer satisfaction rather than a presentation of management committee

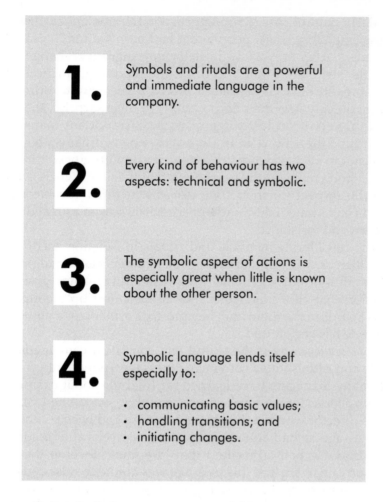

Figure 41 Symbolic language: a powerful language

decisions, he or she is sending a strong and coherent signal about the kind of change it is intended should be achieved in the organization. This change in the agenda is much more than a technical reorganization of agenda items. It is a symbolic expression of a different management style. If the newcomer then also succeeds in resisting the attempts to restore the accustomed order of the items on the agenda, it becomes clear to the employees that he or she has other priorities.

The message you want to send	Your behaviour
'We deal with each other unbureaucratically.'	• Pick up the phone and deal with the matter immediately. • Make pragmatic decisions on the spot.
'We are responsive.'	• Often take telephone calls personally. • Respond to enquiries quickly.
'We value our employees above everything.'	• Greet employees by name. • Remember employee birthdays. • Listen to employee requests and respond.
'The team is important.'	• Have regular meetings and don't cancel them for more important business. • Celebrate achievements with the team. • Stimulate open discussions and knowledge sharing.
'We are flexible and welcome change.'	• Change seating orders and strategies for finding solutions. • Question the way things are routinely done.

Figure 42 Symbolic action at work

The symbolic aspect of actions is exceptionally great during leadership transitions. The employees still know little about the newcomer's values and management style, so each action is subject to multiple interpretations. Managers who pay attention to the symbolism of their actions not only avoid unnecessary resistance and scepticism, but they can selectively use the language of the symbols and rituals to emphasize and support their messages and intentions. After all, symbols and rituals have the fascinating property of speaking to people in an emotional and therefore much more inclusive way than purely 'objective' communication. Hence, they are ideal ways for managers to communicate basic values, establish their standpoints and initiate change.

Changes of leadership entail a wide range of situations in which the language of symbols can be put to particularly effective use, as when the incoming manager wants to:

- establish a strong presence and clarify the nature of the relationship to the predecessor;

- demonstrate the new management values and style and stimulate a cooperative approach;

- communicate security and acceptance;

- develop a new message; and

- facilitate the transition to a new management style and culture.

RITUALS OF TRANSITION AND CHANGE

During a change in leadership, the question that inevitably occupies the employees is: what will change? In their eyes, a change in leadership ultimately signals a transition from an accustomed relationship to a new, still unknown relationship to the boss. Who is that person? What are his or her key values? What will be the main thrusts of the newcomer's work? How does this new boss conceive of cooperation with the employees? What style of leadership does he or she prefer?

Will the new boss do things in exactly the same ways as her direct predecessor, or will she be more like the boss they had several years ago, who started each day by talking with each member of the team individually? In this phase even the slightest changes are noted and interpreted. If the newcomer spends too much time in the office,

The morning ritual of the former boss in a small business in the machine-tool industry is remembered well. He used to appear at 7 am each work day and go straight into his office, where he worked alone, reviewing the important information, which had to be on his desk by the time he arrived. Fully informed, he then began his morning meeting at exactly 9 am in order to coordinate things with his closest employees. The meeting, which was characterized by objectivity and absolute dependability, ended after precisely half an hour.

people immediately ask whether she will be able to understand the reality the sales force faces each day out in the field. If the boss comes from a rival department, people closely watch to see whether her behaviour signals she is going to import the other department's way of dealing with things. Exclusive attention to complaints during the newcomer's first visits to customers may signal that she will always side with the customer rather than back her employees. If she calls employees into her office rather than seeking them out in their own offices, she is likely be seen as an old-fashioned, status-oriented boss. When Louis R Hughes took over as the head of Opel, he wanted to send a strong signal that the leadership culture was to become more team-oriented and less hierarchical. He decided to send the message by eliminating the executive dining room, a move that raised quite a stir. 'It no longer fits our times', he briefly explained.

This example illustrates another aspect of symbolic management. Often, it is not a matter of creating new symbols and rituals but rather only of questioning one's own habits and purposely changing them. This is even more relevant in international leadership transitions where behaviours can take on a completely different meaning without the new manager noticing. In *Saving the Sun: A Wall Street gamble to rescue Japan from its trillion-dollar meltdown* (Duke University Press, 2003), Gillian Tett tells the story of US senior managers arriving at a Japanese bank for the first meeting after they had acquired it:

Collins liked to pride himself in having the common touch... he liked to go around shaking the workers' hands... he hoped this would work in Japan as well... What the Americans did not know was that until then visitors were always shepherded away from the 'private' eating space to special 'guest' rooms... and everybody was supposed to keep to their allotted place... The image of victorious American soldiers stomping into Tokyo after the war... was etched on Japan's cultural memory and explains the reaction to Collins' symbolic acts: 'I guess the new invaders have arrived.'

If you want openness, then closely examine your own habits of dealing with information. If you value personal responsibility, consistently ask your employees for their opinion before answering questions. If you intend to promote flexibility, then you should demonstrate flexible habits yourself. If you value your customers, you should set aside one day a month when you would be free to meet them and discuss any problems that they might have.

Answer questions 1 to 6 in the checklist in Figure 43. When you have answered these questions, you should go through them again and think about how you can support each of your statements. For instance, if you want to be open, then check how your assistant's office handles enquiries, when you make time for your employees and when you approach them. Only if you walk the talk, only by really doing what you say you will do, will you gain credibility quickly. For, in the end, credibility comes from the consistency between words and actions.

SYMBOLS AND RITUALS OF A NEW CORPORATE CULTURE

Symbolic action lends itself not only to managing the leadership transition but also to developing a new corporate culture. Remember, giving strong signals for change is an extremely effective way of gaining buy-in for shared goals. Well-designed start-up meetings with a theme that fits the vision not only convey the goals and what has to be done, but also mark a beginning in a visible and emotionally appealing way for everyone.

It is helpful to think about how to support the desired changes by introducing new rituals, especially when you are asking your

1. How would I describe the ideal manager–employee relationship we should strive for in this organization?

2. How do I think that decisions are best prepared for?

3. How should decisions be made around here?

4. How should people treat each other in this organization?

5. What do I believe are the most important values in the company?

6. What attitude do I expect from my employees?

I will introduce the following rituals to support my management goals and
– see that they are put into practice
– check that they fit the cultural context

Goal: _____
Ritual: _____

Goal: _____
Ritual: _____

Goal: _____
Ritual: _____

Goal: _____
Ritual: _____

Goal: _____
Ritual: _____

Figure 43 Checklist: designing rituals

employees to let go of their deeply ingrained habits and attitudes at work. Such rituals create a sense of security and show people the new desired behaviour.

A ritual of this kind is the greeting mentioned earlier: 'Good afternoon, you are speaking to Ms Miller. What can I do for you?' If the ritual is embedded in a new customer-friendly culture that the employees can understand, it will greatly facilitate the establishment of new behaviour. It reduces the uncertainties about what is appropriate and expected and gives reluctant employees a chance to change. Another way of supporting desired changes is to introduce a simple round of feedback at the end of the regular departmental meetings to see how everyone feels things are working. Such rituals are the reliable building blocks for a new relationship or management style. They afford solid footing and create the space to say things that used to be left unsaid.

It is important, however, that everyone participating in the ritual should fill it with meaning. This is the third principle of symbolic management. The meaning of the ritual unfolds only if the link between it and the overall goal has been successfully communicated to all those involved. The often sceptical attitude towards symbols and rituals comes from the relatively large number of meaningless processes that exist in companies. Lists that are no longer needed, seating arrangements in conferences, distribution lists for invitations to meetings, opening addresses and birthday celebrations are all typical examples of dead rituals. There is hardly any place in which rituals lose their meaning as quickly as in the rapidly changing business world.

1. Which desired changes will be especially difficult for the employees or will conflict with past habits?

2. Which kind of rituals can be used to build a platform for the changes I want to introduce?

3. How can I clearly make the link between my vision and the rituals?

4. Which past rituals will undermine my intentions and will therefore have to change?

Figure 44 Checklist: using rituals

1. Symbols and rituals create credibility, underline important messages and support the process of change.

2. The less the other person knows about me, the greater the symbolic aspect of my actions is.

3. Symbols and rituals should not be looked at in isolation from one another; they must be skilfully combined.

4. Often it is not a matter of coming up with new symbols and rituals but only of enquiring into one's own habits.

5. Symbols and rituals are effective only if they are embedded in the overall context. Their meaning is constantly in danger of being lost.

Some typical mistakes to avoid:

- transferring symbols and rituals from your previous company or job without adaptation;
- saying one thing and doing another;
- starting a ritual without making sure it can be maintained.

Figure 45 Summary of Building Block 7

Part II

Seven case studies illustrating successful leadership transition

Case Study 1

The internal promotion

Kristian is in his late forties. He is a mechanical engineer by training and has been a well-paid technical expert in a major trading company for 20 years. He knows his area and his customers, and works well with the six other experts in the region.

Rumours started to surface that a structural change was pending. There was discussion about new strategies and consulting concepts in which sales were to be better integrated than in the past. Many companies were introducing such changes, and the resulting demands on seasoned employees were high. There was surprise when the new strategy was unveiled a few months later. In a departure from the old structure, the new strategy was to be linked to decentralization. The individual regions were to be run as profit centres, each the responsibility of one manager. The experts in the region were perplexed. They had been working well together for years, so how and why should things suddenly change? Above all, who was to become the new boss? Would it be someone from outside or would one of them move up the ladder?

At first they decided to oppose the structural change, emphasizing their satisfaction with the current situation and arguing that it would be difficult to designate a director among such highly paid employees in such a highly differentiated business. Some of them even announced they would look around for a different company to work for if the new concept were implemented. The regional director stood her ground, though, and encouraged them to apply for the newly created position. When none of them did, she approached Kristian and succeeded in persuading him that it would be logical for his career development to take over as head of his region. Kristian eventually agreed.

His colleagues had nothing against him. On the contrary, they knew of his critical stance towards the new strategy and were glad that someone new was not being imposed upon them. No one envied him, for all agreed that he would have no advantages, only more work and numerous superfluous contacts with headquarters. Even his salary rise would not compensate for that. In every other way, his colleagues thought, nothing would change. Each of them would continue to work well, and they would keep working well as a team.

For some time, that is just how things did work. Kristian saw himself as the link to headquarters and passed on any news or feedback in a meeting with the team every four weeks. Otherwise, he kept himself in the background, emphasizing that everything would go on as it used to and that they would remain an outstanding team.

The first difficulty arose when Kristian had to convey unwelcome news from headquarters. As so often happens in the field, it was about staying in touch. The technical experts were supposed to be equipped with BlackBerries so that they could be reached more easily and could answer questions 24/7. To Kristian's amazement, his colleagues refused. They did not at all understand that he could support this management view. They expected him to see that it was not necessary. They had managed extremely well thus far and were happy to go without the status of a BlackBerry.

Of course, Kristian sensed that a whole range of reasons lurked behind these arguments. Until recently, he himself had been in that role and knew only too well that his activity in the field was specially privileged in that he could not be monitored. He always felt sorry for his colleagues at headquarters, who were forced to document their work time. This difference of opinion was precisely the problem. He was no longer 'one of us' with the technical experts; he had become 'one of them' because he had come to understand the arguments given by headquarters. He saw that the introduction of BlackBerries was not about control exercised by headquarters but about quicker and more flexible action. He knew that his company would be at a great disadvantage if other companies deployed their technical experts faster. He also understood that he, as director, had to put this innovation into practice.

THE INITIAL SITUATION: 'IT'S GOOD THAT NOTHING HAS CHANGED'

Of course, this example is extreme. Everyone knows it is a special challenge suddenly to take charge of a team after many years of working alongside colleagues in the team. But the example above brings to light the situation in which managers often find themselves when they rise to a position of leadership from the ranks.

The employees know their new boss and, for all the ambivalence they may experience upon his or her designation, they are usually happy that their colleague has received the position and not someone else. After all, 'He [She] knows our concerns.' They assume that the new boss can properly stand up for them. They ordinarily expect continuity and a buffer shielding them from serious changes. They tend to forget that a new role also entails new perspectives.

A variation on this theme plays out when the new manager is one of the youngest employees in the department.

This happened to Giorgio, a 30-year-old accountant whose manager had chosen him over colleagues who were 10 to 15 years older. This boss had seen in the younger man the greatest potential for the structural changes under consideration and for the new climate that was intended. The initial situation was marked by a good deal of scepticism and reservation that Giorgio had not anticipated. The young supervisor had at first assumed that his colleagues, with whom he had previously worked very well, would actively support him in the new role. It took him a while to realize that he had to develop his own leadership position and make the employees understand that he saw his role as an active leader, not just a passive recipient of orders from senior management.

TYPICAL PROBLEMS OF INTERNAL PROMOTIONS

New leaders who have been promoted internally grapple with four typical problems:

- *Clear and visible assumption of the leadership role.* Under the pressure of colleagues' expectations that everything will remain as it is, new bosses who have been promoted to lead their former colleagues tend to avoid clearly taking on the new leadership role. This change is not about making status differences visible by switching from informal to formal forms of address and personal interaction. What we are referring to here is the straightforward and appropriate delegation of work previously performed by the new boss, freeing him or her to fulfil the responsibilities entailed in the leadership role. Managers promoted from within their department often carry on exactly as before, except that they now and then attend departmental meetings and other discussions.

- *Delegation of tasks.* The delegation of tasks is difficult not only because it makes the new role uncomfortably apparent but also because the newly promoted boss well knows from personal experience how pressed his or her former colleagues are. Hence, the new boss usually finds it hard to 'impose' even more tasks upon them. Not until the boss faces up to being constantly over-worked and unable to cope with the management load even by working at the weekend does he or she start systematically dele-gating tasks.

- *Close connection to the department.* A third problem always faced by a manager who has been promoted from within his or her own department is the close connection with that unit. It has impacts not only on interpersonal relations, which may be deep, but also on the analysis of issues. The 'organizational blind spots' of insiders are the classic argument against in-house promotions to leadership positions. Such new leaders find it especially difficult to act on ideas that they know the employees do not endorse.

- *Too much background knowledge.* A fourth problem is the fact that managers who have been promoted internally 'know too much'. The problem is not that having a great amount of insider knowledge is a disadvantage but rather that this knowledge usually lulls the new boss into failing to seek out as much information as possible during the early phase of transition. He or she thereby not only misses the chance to gain new perspectives but also unintentionally fails to prepare the employees for possible changes (see Building Block 5).

Our experience shows that managers who have moved up inside the organization tend to react to expectations and responsibilities quickly and without a systematically developed concept. The disadvantages of such firefighting are covered in Building Block 6.

WHAT CAN YOU DO?

- Speak with your former colleagues frankly about your new duties and delegate tasks. Only then will you be able to assume the leadership role.

- Discuss things with each of your employees individually, especially if you believe you already know a lot. Take time for these discussions with your former colleagues. You not only gain new points of view but also establish yourself in your new role.

- If other employees in your department also applied for your new job, speak openly with them about the situation. Be as objective and as understanding as possible, and explore possibilities for constructive cooperation with them.

- Speak with your boss and people in other departments about issues they think need to be considered and about what is expected of you. These discussions will help you focus on your new leadership role.

- Remember that one of the most difficult tasks is to continue successful work. It calls for constant changes. You should therefore think about what you must do to ensure success.

- State within a reasonable period of time what will remain the same as before and what will change. Place it in a balanced and persuasive set of goals.

- Prepare yourself for the possibility that your employees will be disappointed after an initial phase of going along with you. Don't assume that you will be able to meet all their expectations.

The questions in Figure 46 will help you focus on the key issues.

1. What new tasks must you perform in your new position?

2. What expectations will your employees have to correct?

3. What changes will you find especially difficult?

4. What does the new network of your relationships in the company look like?

5. What are your three most important goals in the first six months?

6. For what changes among your employees must you be prepared?

Figure 46 Questions for the manager who has been promoted internally

Building blocks	The internally promoted manager
1. Managing expectations	Your employees: 'Everything stays just as it is!' Your manager: 'Assert yourself!'
2. Building key relationships	Take a clear leadership role. Be aware of your long-standing relationships with your peers and employees.
3. Analysing the situation	Main problem: the manager coming from the inside knows too much and therefore asks too few questions.
4. Establishing goals	Use your set of goals in order to establish your own position.
5. Fostering a climate for change	Develop the climate by systematically asking questions. Use external advisers.
6. Initiating changes	Send strong signals for change. Give employees responsibility.
7. Using symbols and rituals	Set priorities in daily processes. Change meetings and agendas.

Figure 47 Summary of Case Study 1

Case Study 2

Entrepreneur wanted: the external candidate

Agile, entrepreneurial self-starters and risk takers – these are the kind of people sought by companies today. Thirty-three-year-old Ricarda is precisely this kind of person. She has thus far pursued her career with determination and an eye for the essential. After completing her MBA, she started out as a trainee at a major food store chain and learned to take responsibility for decisions. Quite soon she was promoted to store manager, with a large budgetary responsibility. That period was hard, and many of her peers threw in the towel.

After five years she left the company. She knew that she could stand on her own feet and could successfully lead with little support. But she did not want to work in isolation; she wanted to learn something from others. She therefore chose to go into production management at a consumer goods manufacturer. It was there that she experienced for the first time what it means to change from one corporate culture to another. She went from a world of fighting alone, rivalries and hard numbers into a world of the team, reflection and creativity. Strategic thinking to ensure long-term success was what was expected of her in the new company.

She needed a good six months to find her way, but compared to the demands facing her today those months now seem like a holiday. After four years Ricarda was recruited to build a new line of business for a major tourism company. She was excited. It seemed to be the perfect job for her because it drew on several aspects of her experience. She knew not only the day-to-day business with the customers but also how to work strategically and how to maintain success. The company offered her a very attractive package. The expectations seemed clear: build the new area as quickly as possible into a profitable business.

When Ricarda started as the newly appointed general manager of this service-sector venture, she had three employees. Preparations had been sound and everyone waited for the new leader to take things forward. She started quickly, coming up with ideas, seeking business partners and working out sales strategies. In only a year the team grew to 25 employees, a feat that in times of scarce personnel resources at the company generated admiration and envy alike.

Ricarda's problem is not the task. Nor is it the 80-hour week she puts in, although that does worry her. The problem, as she explained in our consulting session, is her colleagues. They do not understand her business and tend to obstruct her. She had an argument with an important area manager over what access her employees should have to the manager's distribution channels. Ricarda wanted her team to have as much freedom as possible in pursuing their objectives, a stance with which the area manager did not agree. In recent months Ricarda's business has grown from being a small start-up venture, and many points of friction have arisen in relations with the parent company. These problems threaten to wear down both Ricarda and her young team.

According to Ricarda the problems are keeping her from her actual work. She has even started thinking about quitting the whole business. Because she is being advised to pay attention to corporate rules, she wonders whether this company really wants an entrepreneurial manager with drive and initiative.

Many a story like this one ends with the surprising resignation of the newcomer. Oswald Neuberger, a leading management professor in Germany, doubts whether large companies are able to deal with such managers at all.

THE INITIAL SITUATION OF THE NEWCOMER

Upon closer examination of the initial situation experienced by the external manager in a large company, Neuberger's statement that such people have it hard is indisputably correct, especially when they possess the desirable attributes of entrepreneurial spirit, drive and initiative. Employees in the company often tend to feel threatened by external managers, a response that many newcomers underestimate and that top managers in the company are apt to deny. The very fact of the newcomer having come from outside the company generates reticence towards him or her. Such external recruitment interferes with the classic paths of career development, and in most cases there are internal candidates for the position. Concern is likely to grow about the idea that external recruitment might become the future policy.

A second threat lies in the situation itself. Most companies justifiably pursue a human resource policy that gives preference to internal candidates for motivational reasons. They usually resort to outsiders when the necessary know-how is not available internally. Be it the card business at Lufthansa, alternative energies at the oil companies, or the mobile telephone activities of the automotive industry, external know-how is sought wherever new fields of business are being cultivated.

The problem is that the employees feel threatened by the competition of external professionals and especially by the fact that these outsiders often take high-profile positions in the company. The new fields of business are ultimately supposed to secure the company's future, and in some cases they are starting points for long-term restructuring. The unavoidable, anxious question of colleagues in the company's established lines of business necessarily becomes: 'Is there any future for people like us, who know every square inch of the business?'

If on top of those fears the newcomer is conspicuously more assertive and energetic in pursuing his or her goals than the company's own managers are, just imagine how those managers are likely to begin slowing the outsider down. The obvious successes are quickly declared 'beginner's luck', and unavoidable failures are discussed at length.

TYPICAL PROBLEMS OF THE
EXTERNAL MANAGER

The description of the initial situation suggests where the typical problems lie for people brought into a company from the outside:

- *The discrepancy between what top management expects and what the employees experience.* The first problem confronting the person coming in from the outside is the frequently encountered discrepancy between what top management expects and what colleagues in middle management experience. Whereas the senior managers usually describe the initial situation clearly and expect the newcomer to get things to happen as quickly as possible, the newcomer's peers are generally far more sceptical about the initiatives for change. It is important to take this latent resistance into consideration if unnecessary trouble is to be avoided in the early days.

- *Time pressure and the need to get to know the organization.* A second problem is that the newcomer's desk is usually piled high with things to be done. As a rule, building up a new area, expanding the team and designing strategies demand full attention. At the same time, the newcomer has to learn the ropes in a completely unknown organization. The external manager has to become familiar with the procedures of the organization, its culture and its characteristic problems, all of which is very time-consuming.

- *The lack of an internal network of relationships.* Apart from the absence of knowledge of procedures, the most serious difference between the external manager and the manager recruited from inside is the outsider's lack of helpful relationships in the organization. The external newcomer does not have the network of key contacts that he or she needs in order to follow through successfully on important steps in a change process. The new manager usually relies on the predecessor's contacts, without knowing precisely how far their influence reaches. The development of key relationships takes time, though, for they must first be discovered and then nurtured.

- *The pressure of the external manager's own expectations.* A fourth problem lies in the pressure of the new manager's own expectations. Moving to a new company is usually an important step on the ladder of success. You usually think it over carefully beforehand and have high hopes for it. If in addition you have successfully negotiated an attractive remuneration package, it is likely that you have built up high expectations of your performance, generating a great deal of pressure on yourself. My team and I have found that such pressure can cause an inappropriate level of concentration on the assigned tasks – at the expense of building a viable network of relationships. The result is a vicious circle that usually remains unbroken.

New corporate culture

Contacts, rules
and processes

New job

New strategies
New team

Scepticism of colleagues

'Look around a
bit first.'

Expectations of your boss

'Quickly build a
new business.'

Your own expectations

'I have to
succeed!'

Figure 48 The vicious circle of the new manager from outside

WHAT CAN YOU DO?

- Treat the performance of technical tasks and the building of a viable network of relationships as two equally important responsibilities from the very beginning.

- Ask your boss who you need to include and keep informed as you build your part of the business.

- In all your discussions remember the necessity of getting to know the organization. Investigate its rules and culture: they are important to the company's success.

- Do not shoot from the hip. Changes in leadership, especially for managers who are new to the company, are not sprints but rather long-distance runs.

- Watch out that your new department does not isolate itself too much from the company and especially that it does not develop a separate corporate culture.

- Avoid getting stuck with too many official duties. Many newcomers seeking to bring 'a breath of fresh air' into project groups have become bogged down by such commitments.

Building blocks	The externally hired manager
1. Managing expectations	Expect that you may encounter scepticism and reticence and be seen as a threat.
2. Building key relationships	Place the highest priority on developing relationships with colleagues.
3. Analysing the situation	Ask 'What do I need to know so I can succeed?'
4. Establishing goals	Avoid taking on too many goals and of being positioned as the 'knight in shining armour' who is expected to save the day.
5. Fostering a climate for change	Don't isolate the department from the rest of the company as a means of stimulating change.
6. Initiating changes	Do not move too quickly, for leadership transitions are a long-distance run, not a sprint.
7. Using symbols and rituals	Seek out internal resources as a signal to your people that not all new ideas are found outside.

Figure 49 Summary of Case Study 2

Case Study 3

The big predecessor and the little successor

David had been the director of customer service for 18 years. His working style had made its mark on the business; for customers and employees he was a living example of a consistent, customer-oriented manager. He was available night and day, and a host of successful service concepts had been devised and put into practice during his era. At a huge farewell party given for David when he retired, his successor celebrated him as a 'monument'.

It is no easy job for his successor, a 48-year-old engineer. He, too, is thoroughly experienced in the customer service area, for he was David's deputy for eight years. The employees respect his work, but he has always been overshadowed by David. They doubt whether he can lead and represent the department as effectively as his predecessor. Top management chose David's deputy to succeed him because they simply wanted things to keep on running as smoothly as they had in the past.

THE INITIAL SITUATION: IN THE SHADOW
OF THE PREDECESSOR

Such leadership transitions occur in all companies. Whenever a predecessor has shaped an area over many years, the successor faces a difficult task. A variety of aspects determine what kind of setting the successor enters.

If the predecessor retires and the successor steps up from within the department, the new boss will generally enjoy the acceptance of

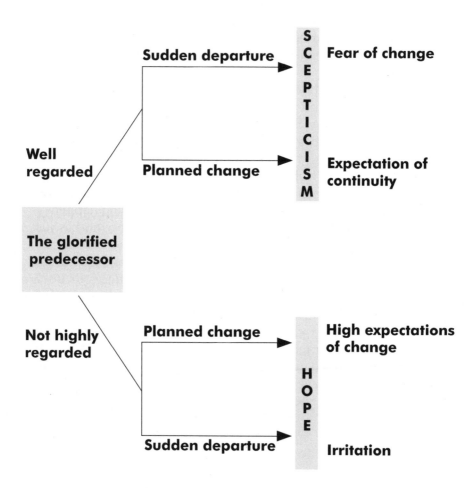

Figure 50 The glorified predecessor and the reactions of the employees

the employees and, hence, will find the initial situation favourable on the whole. The problem, however, is that this successor still stands in the shadow of the predecessor, and it takes time to emerge from it. During the first months, the two leaders – old and new – will be constantly compared to each other by both the successor and, especially, the employees. Often, they cannot even imagine that the former deputy is to become their boss.

Things look altogether different if the 'great' predecessor has suddenly left the company. We experienced a particularly dramatic example in which the predecessor had disagreed with top management and switched to a competitor. She had been very popular with her employees, had worked for the company successfully for more than a decade and had a great deal of influence on structure and strategies. The employees still felt deep loyalty to their former boss when the newcomer arrived. It was a difficult, indeed almost hopeless, situation for him. He came across signs of his predecessor everywhere, and the employees showed little willingness to take his ideas seriously. Some of the employees met him with open disapproval because they assumed that he had had something to do with their former boss's resignation. It took nearly a year before the team started working well with the new boss.

The situation is different yet again when the change in leadership is accompanied by major structural changes. What often happens is that change is long overdue, especially if the person who has just departed had held the position for many years. The successor is expected to make up for lost time and implement changes quickly. In this case the successor is not only compared to the predecessor, but is also measured by whether and how he or she masters the situation.

In this kind of context, the manager coming from outside the company has a better chance than the in-house candidate. The outsider, especially if preceded by a very good reputation, is freer to make changes than the internal candidate, who is closely associated with the way things have been run in the past.

The successor of a 'great' manager always stands in the predecessor's lingering shadow. The degree and intensity of this association depend on the achievements of the predecessor and the amount of time he or she worked for the company.

TYPICAL PROBLEMS OF THE SUCCESSOR

- *Being forever branded as number two.* For the manager who has thus far served as the deputy to a highly regarded predecessor, the main difficulty is that of having been moulded by the role of being 'second', particularly if he or she has had that status for some time. One problem is that the employees cannot even begin to imagine the eternal deputy suddenly taking the lead. Another – and far greater – danger is that the new leader has identified so strongly with the former role of being number two that shedding it is not at all simple. Some former deputies find it hard to envisage what can be changed. Their job until now has been to put into practice what their boss laid out or what had been worked out jointly.

- *The expectations of the employees.* When the deputy becomes the boss, he or she will necessarily behave differently from how he or she behaved in the past. Employees often find it hard to imagine that their former colleague is supposed to change behaviour overnight. They are therefore often confused when the new leader suddenly makes demands or prevails in decisions instead of fulfilling the accustomed function of the go-between.

- *The position in the circle of colleagues.* The third major difficulty for the new manager is to establish a position among his or her peers. The other managers have seen him or her for many years only as the second-in-command, so the shadow of the predecessor accompanies the new manager even into top management meetings. Sometimes it takes a lot of patience not to be offended by frequent questions about the predecessor.

- *The constant comparison to the predecessor.* The externally hired successor of a glorified predecessor stands deep in the latter's shadow. The constant comparisons can become difficult to bear for the external newcomer, who can neither withdraw from conversations about the predecessor's achievements nor take up the 'invitation' to compare him- or herself directly against the predecessor's qualities. The situation can be tricky because, if the successor tries to evade the comparison by not enquiring when the employees speak about their former boss, they may glorify the predecessor all the more.

- *The weaknesses of the great predecessor.* In most cases glorified predecessors occupied their positions for many years, so some structures and procedures will need an overhaul. The successor must avoid falling into the trap of attributing responsibility for the structural problems to the predecessor. This response is indeed a temptation because the dynamics outlined above can lead to circumstances in which it is almost a relief to have at last found a few mistakes committed by the seemingly infallible predecessor. These discoveries can distort how the past is seen and then lead to the inability to appreciate the predecessor's merits.

The successor must understand and accept that the emotional ties between the employees and the predecessor will take a long time to dissolve and that criticism of the former manager's achievements will be hard to accept. Trust in the new leader can emerge only to the degree that the ties to the predecessor loosen and relations normalize over time.

WHAT CAN YOU DO?

- Plan a clean and clear transition. Speak with your predecessor and your future boss about the options you have for managing the handover of business as visibly as possible for all employees.

- See to it that your predecessor is given an appropriate farewell.

- Do not accept the invitation to follow in your predecessor's footsteps. It would be impossible to do justice to that task. Make it clear from the outset that you are a different person and that something new is bound to emerge.

- Be sure to establish yourself clearly in your new position. Speak to your employees and colleagues about their expectations of you as the new boss.

- Show through your actions that you appreciate your predecessor's work. Often we find that the new leader expresses the necessary respect verbally, but then contradicts the message by too hastily changing accustomed routines. Employees pick up very perceptively on gaps between words and behaviour.

- Show interest in the work that has led to success in the past. Ask about important changes and find out what the department is proud of.

- Treat criticism of your predecessor very carefully. As soon as you encourage your employees to criticize your predecessor, you will see that they will immediately distance themselves from you.

- The new leader – whether he or she served as the former second-in-command or came in from a different company – must formulate a clear and, above all, balanced set of goals. This must clearly convey what will change and what will stay the same. Try to strike a good balance between the two.

Building blocks	Moving out of the shadow of the glorified predecessor
1. Managing expectations	Expect either high expectations or the expectation of continuity. Be prepared for constant comparison to the glorified predecessor.
2. Building key relationships	Arrange for an official farewell for the predecessor. Position yourself clearly vis-à-vis colleagues.
3. Analysing the situation	As Guiseppe di Lampedusa said, 'If we want things to stay as they are, things will have to change.'
4. Establishing goals	Formulate goals only after detailed analysis with the team, if possible.
5. Fostering a climate for change	Beware of taboo issues. Avoid making changes too hastily.
6. Initiating changes	Include the employees in the process. Send clear signals for change.
7. Using symbols and rituals	Show respect for your predecessor. Establish new signs and symbols.

Figure 51 Summary of Case Study 3

Case Study 4

The young high-potential manager

A company's young high-flyers who have been designated early for future management responsibilities in the organization constitute a special group. They are chosen in carefully crafted selection procedures and placed together in a small group. They are familiarized with projects and are taken quickly through their first stages of leadership. They often have contact with the higher echelons of management.

What happens when these designated young people take over leadership responsibilities? What expectations will they encounter, and what challenges must they meet?

Laura had graduated from a German university and had gone on to study for an MBA in the United States, where she had established a large number of solid contacts with international companies. After returning to Germany, Laura had been recruited as a trainee in a leading German bank, an organization known for its excellent human resource development.

During her training she worked on numerous projects, and her communication skills, commitment and outstanding analytical abilities very soon drew attention. A member of the managing board became her mentor. Laura's first job after completing the two-year training was as head of a group working on new products. It consisted of five young people who had the job of developing ideas and rolling them out in the branch offices. She gained a great deal of experience during her three years in this job, and she participated in a special management development programme at the bank.

She was then appointed as a branch manager, where she had some significant challenges to deal with. Although it was a small, rural branch, her predecessor had done exceptional work over many years. It was therefore not easy for Laura to gain the acceptance she needed from her employees and the bank's customers. Fortunately, however, she quickly succeeded at establishing communications with her predecessor, who passed on several tips in the first three months. He advised Laura on technical matters and counselled her on how best to deal with the employees. He also helped her develop relationships with the important customers.

'Without the bank's foresight in the transition planning, which gave me enough time to learn the ropes in the new job, and without the support of my predecessor, I probably would not have made it,' Laura commented. 'I still remember how difficult it all was at the beginning. The scepticism from the employees also made it really hard for me. After all, I came from having worked with a team of peers and suddenly had 50-year-olds to contend with.'

The really crucial leadership transition for Laura came three years later. The bank had a sudden vacancy and asked Laura to make the move up to a position as regional manager. The move was unplanned and definitely too early, for at 34 years of age she suddenly had responsibility for five branch offices with 45 employees. The job also meant implementing a strategic reori-entation that would have a significant impact on people in these branches.

These circumstances had almost nothing of what makes a 'good' change in leadership. All but two of Laura's branch managers were 10 to 15 years older than her. One of them had shown a keen interest in the position of regional manager. Moreover, the strategic change had already caused quite a stir, and many employees were unsettled about what was in store for them. It came as a shock when it was announced that Laura was to take over the position. Most of the employees doubted that such a young manager was up to the task.

The first months were extremely difficult. 'I will never forget my first meeting with the branch managers. Although I was used to dealing with scepticism, I had never experienced anything like what I faced there. Eight people sat reserved and silent before me, and every attempt on my part to loosen up the situation failed. The branch manager who had been interested in my position was the only one who asked questions. It took more than three months of hard work for the atmosphere to thaw a bit. During that period I thought at times about giving up, and my husband was really worried. I had heart problems for the first time in my life and risked losing my optimistic outlook.'

THE INITIAL SITUATION: SCEPTICISM AND RESERVE

The dynamic of the situation that Laura faced is typical of a leadership involving high-potential managers. My team and I have observed it in many companies. Such a difficult initial situation does not arise with the first assignment; it tends to occur after the manager has climbed a couple of steps on the career ladder in quick succession.

The predicament is almost always characterized by great scepticism on the part of the employees as to whether the young manager can even begin to handle the new job. Expressed more or less openly, this scepticism drains energy from the momentum needed in a transition. Rumours that make life unnecessarily hard for the newcomer quickly circulate: 'The new boss must have good connections' or 'You only have to have the right mentor around here.'

Things become especially problematic if there is also a hidden competitor among the employees. After all, it is much simpler to lose out in the competition for a promotion if the job goes to a seasoned manager than if a young one with less experience wins the position. The initial situation in the transition tends to be that the employees are sceptical and reserved and that the newcomer is insecure and isolated.

TYPICAL PROBLEMS OF THE HIGH-POTENTIAL MANAGER

- *Being perceived as purely career-oriented.* Because many young managers are unaccustomed to dealing with such scepticism and aloofness, they tend to retreat into 'objective' or 'businesslike mode' rather than working in 'human mode'. Newcomers who are otherwise always open and expressive become cautious and reserved. Unsure about how much of their personality they can allow to show in the unwelcoming office environment, newcomers work particularly conscientiously. The problem is that this strategy ends up unwittingly feeding the conjectures that they have no interest in the people around them. The employees feel confirmed in their assumption that their new manager is thinking only of his or her career.

- *Being overly dependent on the boss.* A second effect young managers have to battle with is that such transitions magnify their dependence on the boss, from whom they seek advice and support for dealing with the problems they face at the outset. That relationship, however, inevitably increases the distance from the employees, who observe young high-potential managers especially carefully and critically. They want to know whether the newcomer identifies more with 'us down here' or 'them up there'.

- *Denying normal insecurities.* A major problem for such young managers in the initial situation is that they understandably try to hide their insecurities, which always exist. This behaviour inhibits interaction with the employees, making everything quite stiff and formal. Usually things do not improve and normalize until the new manager has actually faced up to his or her insecurities and shown a human side.

- *Dealing with gaps in expertise.* Because young high-potential managers lack some of the necessary experience and knowledge for their new position, they are dependent on the expertise of their older employees. It is therefore particularly important for young managers to make the effort to establish and maintain good working relationships with experienced employees in order to make the necessary decisions. One of the biggest mistakes some young high-potential managers make is to try to rely solely on their own expertise.

WHAT CAN YOU DO?

- The first thing that you need to do as a young manager in such a situation is to become aware of these dynamics.

- Despite the reserve and scepticism that you encounter, you should work consistently on the key relationships from the outset. Speak to your hidden competitor, find out about your team's abilities and be open in the way you deal with the employees. The point is to show that you are a human being and that you care about people, not just the task at hand.

- Enquire into the strengths of your team and include them in your decisions.

- Make it clear that you are intent not only on scoring success as quickly as possible but also on giving high priority to your employees' long-term interests.

- Develop a set of goals, taking care that they, too, reflect issues of long-term importance to the employees.

Building blocks	The high-potential manager
1. Managing expectations	Be prepared for responses to range from scepticism to aloofness and reserve.
2. Building key relationships	Be aware of hidden competitors and informal leaders.
3. Analysing the situation	Diagnose problems together with your employees and emphasize strengths.
4. Establishing goals	Consider your employees' long-term interests.
5. Fostering a climate for change	Build up resources and behave confidently.
6. Initiating changes	Don't undertake too many changes, and don't expect too much of yourself.
7. Using symbols and rituals	Initiate conversations, let people know who you are and show that you respect what they have accomplished.

Figure 52 Summary of Case Study 4

Case Study 5

The long-drawn-out start

Michael is the successful head of a project in an industrial company. He is in his early thirties and enjoys a reputation as a 'go-getter' – goal-driven, yet personable. Top management appreciates his proactive style of leadership and expects that he will go far in the company.

He has been offered a position as head of a different department within the company. It would mean leaving sales and going to a factory at another location to take over the logistics function there. This assignment would not only entail a change of location for Michael, but it would be a highly unusual career move for two reasons. Logistics has a poor reputation in the company, and it is rare for managers to move from headquarters to a factory (and vice versa). The two parts of the organization keep each other at arm's length and disparage each other's performance. It is no easy task for people to move from one part of the business to the other and become integrated.

Nonetheless, Michael has decided to accept the position, which he sees as a big step forward in his career. The new task intrigues him, for the director of the factory wants to reorient the logistics area, which is currently not very efficient. Michael has a clear mandate for change. Profitability must increase, and he is tasked with completely restructuring the function. The assignment is scheduled to start on 1 April, but Michael arrives on 1 March to get his bearings in the factory.

However, when Michael arrives he is not officially presented as the future head of the department, and his function is unclear to the employees. Rumours circulate that he will succeed Arnold, for whom the company has not yet found a position and who continues in his job as the head of logistics. Arnold shows little enthusiasm for the newcomer and boycotts his integration. Michael throws himself into his first project, which is designed to familiarize him with the logistics area. In the first weeks, he is to examine the area, analyse processes and ascertain potential synergies. Michael is convinced that he can see where changes need to be made, and he is sure that he can position himself again as a 'doer'. The responsibility for the turnaround project does not help him integrate into the organization, nor does his previous reputation as a tough manager. As a result, the employees become increasingly anxious.

As 1 April approaches, top management postpone Michael's official transition to the position of departmental head, leaving it with Arnold, for whom a new assignment still has not been found. Michael continues his project. But he has almost no support. Having come from headquarters, he has no network to draw on in the factory. Michael receives no information about a firm date on which he will officially start. The procedure for putting the organizational change process in motion remains unclear.

Four months later Arnold still has not left the department. He continues to occupy Michael's future office. The situation remains confusing and ambiguous for all concerned: Michael, his predecessor and the employees. It is increasingly unlikely that the new department will experience a positive 'new beginning' with Michael when he takes over officially and launches the restructuring process. Michael threatens to resign before he even starts.

THE INITIAL SITUATION:
THE LONG-DRAWN-OUT START

A change in leadership in which the predecessor still performs the newcomer's designated function can certainly offer advantages – if the situation is clear, if all employees are informed and if the lines of authority and the moment of the handover are defined. Under those conditions the incoming manager can learn a great deal from his or her predecessor (including what might be done differently). The newcomer can establish a clear position, learn about the history of any issues, set the course for future responsibilities and send the right messages. In contrast, if the situation surrounding the handover is not clearly managed, or if the incumbent and the successor are professionally at odds with each other, the start threatens to become protracted. Even before the new manager takes over, his or her credibility has been damaged and position weakened.

This kind of start is in many ways very problematic for the employees as well. It is unclear to them whether a change in leadership will really happen and who will actually be their boss. An equally great burden is the anxiety and uncertainty of wondering what other changes will take place under a new boss.

The above example of a long-drawn-out start is not unique. Such a beginning is especially risky for the successor if there is little chance of cooperation with the predecessor and perhaps not even a table to work at. In this situation the incoming manager has to focus on using time effectively without becoming involved in technical issues and without prematurely jockeying for position. It is important to analyse the initial situation constructively and inconspicuously and to avoid taking on any management responsibilities. The task under these circumstances is to become familiar with the organization's culture, to learn its rules and social architecture and to get a feeling for how people will deal with change, for example whether they are open to it and whether they have the necessary skills.

In the situation depicted in this case study, additional problems are triggered by the employees' fears of restructuring and by Michael's reputation from his previous job. Furthermore, Michael comes from a part of the company that is unpopular in the department to which he is transferring. His start is increasingly perceived as a threat, and he is seen as an outsider.

During the period before officially beginning in the new function, Michael commits a major mistake by not investing in the development of relationships. Instead, he focuses solely on the analytical aspects of his project. But building key relationships is crucial in a leadership transition, especially for the changes he has in mind. Having a network of contacts in the organization is essential to enabling the new manager to know how to leverage change and where to draw on the support needed for implementing change.

The next minefield in the transition process comes when the newcomer at last officially takes the management position. The interaction with the predecessor and the employees requires great sensitivity. Everyone needs to see a clear sign of commitment from top management to the new boss. The employees should be informed about the newcomer's plans and visions in a well-designed launch event. The moment must really be made to feel like a new beginning for everyone (see Figure 53).

The transition workshop

Successful leadership transitions depend on how rapidly the team and the new leader come to work efficiently together. Transition workshops shorten the time needed for the manager to build a cooperative relationship with the team. Such workshops facilitate dialogue between people at different hierarchical levels, and they are powerful symbolic instruments for communicating a change in leadership style.

During the first weeks of the leadership transition, there are many unanswered questions in the minds of employees. A transition workshop uses this curiosity-driven energy to build solid working relations between the new boss and the members of the team and to establish a constructive climate. Promoting trust and a forward-looking approach is crucial, particularly when significant changes must be launched in the organization, for which strong employee commitment is needed.

Goals

- Clarify mutual expectations.
- Identify the employees' strengths.
- Accelerate the team-building process.
- Cultivate a positive climate for change.
- Develop a shared understanding of the relevant issues.
- Focus the team on common goals.

Figure 53 The transition workshop

The farewell and respect given to the predecessor are equally important. Both gestures are liable to be partly undermined by a long-drawn-out start. A predecessor whose departure is not treated with the appropriate respect quickly comes to be seen as a martyr.

TYPICAL PROBLEMS OF THE LONG-DRAWN-OUT START

The example in this case study shows the typical challenges brought about by a long-drawn-out start:

- *Dealing with management's ambiguous messages and protracted decisions.* When the start in a position of leadership is delayed, the newcomer must strike a delicate balance between making a determined, resolute entry on the one hand and showing flexibility and a willingness to learn on the other. It is very important to draw clear boundaries around the responsibilities in order to avoid being exploited, and it is equally important to ensure that no one loses face during the protracted transition process.

- *Balancing between attending to tasks and attending to relationships.* A typical intuitive transition strategy is the early priority of getting to know the key facts, important work processes and 'problems to fix'. Rather than meeting people and making his or her presence felt, the new manager stays in the office to 'get on top of the work'. The next step in this strategy shows up the imbalanced approach, when solutions are needed for implementation. Goodwill suffers as people are disappointed in the apparent lack of interest in their views and what they have to offer.

- *Beginning in the new position and giving a send-off to the predecessor.* Although not easy to manage in a protracted transition, the newcomer's start must mark a definite new beginning. The risk of offending the predecessor is best avoided by publicly honouring the predecessor's achievements and past significance. The farewell to the predecessor then becomes a clear signal for the successor's start. This gesture must be unequivocal: this stage belongs to the predecessor.

WHAT CAN YOU DO?

- Use the time leading up to the start as an opportunity to learn about the organization, and do not perform any active management functions.

- Before you start your new position officially, avoid excessive professional, technical involvement and invest in developing key relationships from the outset.

- Clarify your expectations with your boss. Discuss and plan the official, visible handover procedure with your boss and your predecessor.

- Build team spirit. Successful restructuring requires a constructive climate for change and emotional connection with the employees. An off-site workshop, for example, can be a useful way to launch a new phase of team building.

- Arrange a respectful farewell event for your predecessor, one that neither diminishes the regard in which the predecessor is held nor elevates him or her to the status of martyr. Deal cautiously with any criticism of your predecessor, both while the predecessor is still around and after he or she has left.

- Formulate a set of goals that energize your employees, and pursue the most important goals resolutely.

Building blocks	The long-drawn-out start
1. Managing expectations	Be prepared for scepticism and perplexity.
2. Building key relationships	Ensure that affairs are clearly handed on from your predecessor to you.
3. Analysing the situation	See the situation through the eyes of your employees and the key players in the organization.
4. Establishing goals	Formulate a persuasive set of goals by the time you begin, and pursue the most important goals steadily after you start in your new position.
5. Fostering a climate for change	Show appreciation for your employees and foster open communication with them.
6. Initiating changes	Give clear signals for a new start and delegate tasks and responsibilities for making it happen.
7. Using symbols and rituals	Do not disparage your predecessor. Use start-up rituals to show how you want to manage.

Figure 54 Summary of Case Study 5

Case Study 6

The assignment abroad

Philip has been promoted to head of the marketing department in an Italian subsidiary. The change is seen as an opportunity to restructure marketing and especially as a chance to pull together the company's international marketing activities. Past attempts to integrate what is being done in the various countries have had little success. The activities in Italy in particular have been too isolated from those in the rest of the company.

For Philip, this new task area is a meaningful step in his career development. The members of his family also see it positively. They have spent several holidays in Italy, so the country seems familiar to them, and they can easily imagine living there for a while. The children are four and six years old, so their integration is not likely to be difficult. The company will help find a house and sort out other matters of getting settled in the new environment.

The reception in Italy is friendly, though Philip can sense that the Italian employees are asking themselves whether a US manager really is able to run marketing campaigns in their country. In initial discussions, Philip encounters self-assured colleagues who describe to him in great detail the special characteristics of the Italian market. He is repeatedly asked what his idea of successful marketing is and how he intends to proceed. He responds to such questions by pointing out that he first has to get an impression of the situation before he can say where things are headed.

Three weeks later, the situation has already changed considerably. Philip has had many discussions and has meanwhile built himself a pretty clear picture of the situation. He is no longer surprised that it has been impossible to agree on joint strategies. Almost all the suggestions and ideas from the United States are immediately rejected by his Italian colleagues. However, he also realizes that the ideas have been presented in a way that has made it difficult for the Italians to accept them. He senses from his employees a growing scepticism about his proposals, behind all of which they suspect an attempt to make typically US approaches prevail. Two of his key team members have already received attractive offers from other companies and have indicated they are likely to change jobs soon.

THE INITIAL SITUATION: THE EXPATRIATE

The case depicted above is a typical example of an international leadership transition. A description of the hurdles Philip will face in the coming months would fill many pages. Looking back, nearly all expatriates report that they underestimated the cultural differences, especially those between countries that seem similar at first glance. The constant tension with their role as ambassador from the home company also made life difficult for them, as did the scepticism engendered by that perception. Moreover, the styles of leadership differed, the networks were opaque, and language problems got in the way of good communication. Experience shows that the families, too, go through a crisis after a 'honeymoon' at the beginning of the stay abroad.

International assignments almost always involve initiating change, so the expatriate is usually under high pressure right from the start. Careful preparation is therefore becoming ever more important. The newcomer must prepare for the typical intercultural adjustments that lie in store and must focus particularly on the management situation.

Many companies used to treat expatriate assignments primarily as a development opportunity. Managers were sent abroad, usually for two years, to gain international experience in preparation for future global functions. Everyone involved knew it would be a temporary stay that would not entail any significant changes for the local organization. An advantage of this arrangement was that it avoided placing undue pressure on expatriates, who could then legitimately take time to get their bearings and familiarize themselves with their surroundings. Today, however, most companies give their expatriate managers responsibility for changing structures, policies or procedures in their new location. The expatriate assignment is therefore more demanding than it used to be.

Every expatriate needs to be aware that adaptation to the host country's conventions of communication is important for developing positive working relations. Even though English has become the dominant language in international business, the ability to use even a few expressions in the local language will be appreciated as a sign that the newcomer is interested in adapting to the foreign culture. Going further and becoming initiated into the conventions of social encounters usually opens doors to personal relations that help overcome early difficulties.

There is yet another aspect to consider when it comes to cultural adaptation. Many behaviours that seem simple to change are deeply anchored in national character, so it is very problematic to expect people to adopt behaviours that contradict their traditions and values. For example, it is almost inconceivable for a Japanese manager to engage in the 'open discussion' that Westerners value so highly. The Japanese concern about offending someone else is so culturally ingrained this it is probably all but insurmountable. However, tensions can build because of smaller differences, too – for example, the tendency of US businesspeople to describe even serious problems in positive terms as 'challenges' tends to irritate their German colleagues, for whom 'problem solving' is evidence of professional expertise.

It is therefore always a good idea, especially in the early phase, for the expatriate manager to piece together as objective a picture as possible of the cultural habits that shape the new work environment. The most important aspects to pay attention to are communication style and conflict behaviour, especially how colleagues interact with one another, how they deal with differences in status and how they share information.

Dimension	Way in which demonstrated	
Management style	Experts	←→ General manager
Status	Based on competence	←→ Based on background
Development of relationships	Reserved formal	←→ Direct informal
Relations with colleagues	Reserved	←→ Personal
Conflict behaviour	Frank, direct, confrontational	←→ Indirect, avoiding confrontation
Presentation of ideas	From the specific to the general	←→ From the general to the particular
Social orientation	Individualist	←→ Collectivist

Figure 55 A few differences you should know about

TYPICAL PROBLEMS FOR THE EXPATRIATE

I definitely underestimated cultural differences.
(Expatriate after a year and a half abroad)

Philip's case illustrates a few basic issues that can await an expatriate:

- *Increased importance of the need to clarify the assignment.* Important
  as careful clarification of assignments is in leadership transitions
  within the manager's own country, it becomes utterly crucial
  when transfer to a foreign country is involved. Especially in this
  era of constant change, the new management assignment is
  bound to involve initiating some change. All too often, however,
  the expectations are not formulated explicitly. If managers do not
  have a clear sense of the kind of changes they will be expected to
  achieve and if they do not consciously decide which change
  objectives they will commit themselves to delivering, the expatriate transition can become extremely difficult. The often
  complicated legal issues between the foreign subsidiary and
  headquarters frequently lead to additional difficulties that the
  expatriate manager must deal with.

- *Increased importance of the orientation phase and leadership transition
  rituals.* Experience has shown that expatriate managers need
  twice the amount of time for the transition phase as managers
  who take a new leadership role within their home countries. This
  difference is due not only to the fact that it takes considerably
  longer for expatriates to find their bearings in the foreign setting,
  but also to the expectations of the new setting. In many countries
  managers find that they are expected to invest in developing
  personal relationships before getting down to business. This is
  true of most Asian cultures, as well as the United States and
  southern European countries such as France, Spain and Italy.
  The invitation to dinner in France, the welcome party in the
  United States and the first cordial conversations in Japan – they
  are all rituals of relationship building that are not to be blithely
  ignored. If the expatriate does not take these rituals seriously
  and instead chooses to get straight down to business, local

managers are likely to take offence and the business relationship will suffer as a result.

- *The response to cultural differences.* Although repeatedly denied by many managers, except those transferred to Asian countries, the shift to life as an expatriate always means confronting cultural differences. What usually makes life difficult for expatriates is not the immediately obvious differences such as friendliness, manner and discussion style but rather the differences in mentality. These underlying, but very important, differences generally become apparent to the newcomer after a certain period of acclimatization.

- *Increased importance of the situation to the family, spouse or partner.* Studies show that most failures of expatriate transfers are due not to occupational hardships but to problems with the family, spouse or partner. Usually the pressure to adapt to the foreign setting is even greater for them than for the new manager, and after about three months a crisis looms. If both members of dual-career couples undergo the stress of transition to a new job in a new country at the same time, the problems may escalate at home, sometimes leading to the premature termination of the assignment. Planning of the move abroad from the personal perspective therefore deserves special attention.

WHAT CAN YOU DO?

- Thoroughly prepare for the new assignment, the country and the new culture. Actively include your family in this. Attending a seminar on the special characteristics of the country is helpful but usually not sufficient. It is recommended that you take an initial family trip to the new country, where you can also gather information on the expectations of your future bosses, colleagues and employees as well as learn about their experiences to date.

- When you start the new position, devote the necessary attention not only to relationships but also to your cultural adaptation. All future employees and colleagues will watch to see how you present yourself and how far you adapt to the customs and conventions of the country. They will try to read from your behaviour how interested you are in engaging with their culture.

- Pay particular attention to the orientation phase. As an expatriate, you should enquire into expectations, important issues and key relationships and devote the necessary attention to the cultural rules of the game. It is often just as important to understand the country and its people as it is to decode the specific business situation you are in.

- After two or three months, reflect on your experience. In that time many managers begin to build up personal resistance to the foreign culture. This response goes almost unnoticed and is a natural reaction to the constant confrontation with customs and habits that are often incomprehensible. The problem is that this reaction, often expressed by the expatriate manager as 'Well, I am simply different' or 'It does not make sense anyway', is liable to lead to misunderstandings and communication problems.

What appears similar at first glance harbours essential differences in detail

- *Both countries have the issue of leadership*, but in Germany managers are expected to be strong decision-makers and competent specialists, whereas in the United States managers see themselves primarily as problem-solvers.

- *Both countries demand personal responsibility*, but Americans are convinced that they control their own destiny, whereas in Germany external circumstances are taken into greater consideration.

- *Both countries are forward looking*, but for Americans the future is like a magnet, whereas Germans grapple more with the present situation.

- *Both countries emphasize career and success*, but Germans attach more importance to having a secure job and the associated social contacts, whereas Americans focus more on success.

- *Both countries value relationships*, but how people develop them and how much they expect from them is very different.

Figure 56 Some intercultural differences between the United States and Germany

Building blocks	The expatriate
1. Managing expectations	Prepare well for the stay abroad, and try to learn a few things about the country and its people.
2. Building key relationships	Use the first weeks for building relationships. Discover the cultural rules of the game, and include your family in this learning.
3. Analysing the situation	Analyse the initial situation with special care, and get your bearings in the foreign country and the culture.
4. Establishing goals	Develop a carefully planned set of goals appropriate to the market and the new country.
5. Fostering a climate for change	Attend to both one-to-one relationships and cultural adaptation.
6. Initiating changes	Be sure that your plan for change takes into account the likely distrust in your ability to understand the local conditions.
7. Using symbols and rituals	Do not represent only the interests of headquarters, and do not seek information only from the expatriates of your home country.

Figure 57 Summary of Case Study 6

Case Study 7

Learning at headquarters: the challenge to managers from foreign subsidiaries

Wu Chang is considered a high-potential manager in a Chinese company that belongs to a British multinational group. His boss and the human resource director believe that he is a possible candidate for the next management level. Wu Chang has been working in the purchasing department for five years, and as a 34-year-old he no longer has much time left to make a career jump. In China, any rise to the higher levels of management is expected by the age of 36. To advance, however, Wu Chang needs international management competence, which he does not have.

Wu Chang's boss succeeds in arranging an assignment for him at corporate headquarters in the UK. Wu Chang therefore goes to Birmingham to lead a project intended to improve the integration of the Asian business divisions into the company structure. Wu Chang's personal goal for this assignment is to be promoted during his stay at headquarters, because his Chinese boss has told him he will be promoted after his return only if he has earned a promotion in the UK.

The company helps Wu Chang to find a flat in Birmingham and to complete the bureaucratic formalities, and his new team cordially receives him. He comes to realize, though, that he cannot expect much substantive support for his project from either his boss or his colleagues, because they have little or no knowledge of the Asian market.

In this new assignment Wu Chang bears heavy responsibility for making the expected changes, and he is pressed to begin as quickly as possible. He needs the cooperation of his British colleagues in order to accomplish the task, which calls for political competence and rapid integration into company headquarters.

Although Wu Chang is highly motivated and, as an expert, well equipped with the know-how necessary for this conceptual work, the task gives him problems. The biggest difficulties for him lie in the European work mentality. He finds it hard to understand the decision-making processes of the British headquarters and the European mindset. Although he has a strong network in China, he does not know how to build one in the European context. Moreover, he does not understand the power structure in headquarters. The fact that he came in from a foreign subsidiary does not make the situation any easier for him. He has doubts about his standing at headquarters, the professional competence attributed to him, and his own performance.

THE INITIAL SITUATION: THE MANAGER FROM A FOREIGN SUBSIDIARY

Companies have a long-standing practice of sending out managers from headquarters. Only recently, however, have many companies started moving managers in the opposite direction, namely from foreign subsidiaries to headquarters. The challenges faced by these managers from foreign subsidiaries are similar to those faced by expatriates, but important differences make it worthwhile to treat their special situation separately here.

The assignment of the manager from a foreign subsidiary in the situation outlined above is clear, but many managers do not have the advantage of such a well-defined objective. Far too often the newcomer is not given a clear function and must invest a great deal of time in identifying the specific contribution that is expected. Such confusion is bound to lead to dissatisfaction and frustration.

A clear assignment to change procedures between headquarters and foreign subsidiaries is a very tough challenge. In the present case, the task is to restructure business processes or to coordinate global procedures. New managers like Wu Chang arrive from abroad and step into the headquarters job with explicit instructions to start as quickly as possible. Not surprisingly, managers from foreign subsidiaries in this situation find that they have little time left over to adjust to the cultural setting and to build functioning networks. This adaptation puts a double burden and tremendous pressure to perform on managers from foreign subsidiaries because they must find their way in an unfamiliar professional situation while dealing with the challenge of trying to understand the foreign culture. A further complicating factor is that the manager's identity – habits, behaviours and views – is confronted by the cultural expectations of the new country and the company. Great flexibility is therefore one of the most important characteristics required of managers who make international leadership transitions. They need such flexibility in order to adapt to the corporate and social settings into which they move.

The foreign manager's leadership transition is made even more difficult by a particular kind of competition with the host-country colleagues. Everyone involved knows that the foreign manager is staying only temporarily. Managers from foreign subsidiaries usually come to headquarters to assimilate know-how for no more than three years. Managers then take back to their subsidiaries the competence necessary for independently carrying out tasks previously managed by headquarters. In other words, they start doing this work in their own country. Hence, colleagues at headquarters do not necessarily always want to see a manager from a foreign subsidiary successfully learn from them.

Managers from foreign subsidiaries run a career risk by leaving their country and moving to headquarters. Their goal is to develop a career in the subsidiary after returning from headquarters, but the long absence from the subsidiary may jeopardize precisely that career path.

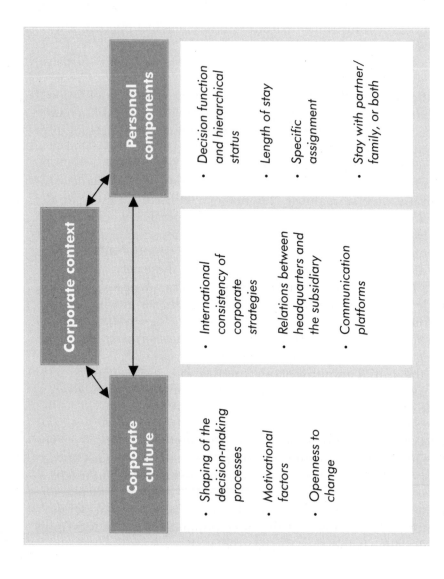

Figure 58 Factors of successful international leadership transitions

TYPICAL PROBLEMS OF THE MANAGER FROM A FOREIGN SUBSIDIARY

It takes a long time to understand decision making and power structures.
(Manager from a foreign subsidiary, after a year in Germany)

Making a leadership transition takes courage, and international comparison shows it to be especially difficult when that change means moving to a country with rigid regulations. Managers from foreign subsidiaries in Germany, for example, often say that it is difficult to find their way in the bureaucratic jungle.

In addition, many countries are not homogeneous, but made up of culturally diverse regions. This makes it difficult to give simple, clear advice that applies throughout the country. Each region in such countries has its own closed networks, making it difficult even for national transfers. A manager from another country will therefore have an even harder time becoming a part of these networks.

The fact is that few countries are especially adept at integrating people from other cultures. It is easier in countries in which a large international community has formed, and well-established networks for workers from other countries support managers during their leadership transition process.

In the initial months of acclimatization, a great number of surprises and problems can await managers from foreign subsidiaries:

- *Lack of an effective network of relationships at headquarters.* The manager from a foreign subsidiary does not have the network of key relationships needed successfully to take important steps in the process of change at headquarters. He or she usually relies on the boss's contacts, without knowing how far that person's influence extends. But the development of key relationships takes time before they can be used at all.

- *Difficult intercultural cooperation and latent competition.* The frequently entangled relations between headquarters and the subsidiaries lead to complications in many cases. Moreover, local colleagues at headquarters frequently perceive the manager from the foreign subsidiary as a future rival because they may be concerned that they will lose their own responsibilities and competencies to the foreign subsidiary when the manager returns to his or her country.

- *Strain on private life.* Experience shows that partners and families have the most adapting to do in the new setting. In many cases they are not sufficiently involved in the planning and preparation for the move to the new country.

- *Bureaucracy and culture shock.* Managers from foreign subsidiaries often encounter important and sometimes difficult and challenging issues and situations in setting up life outside the company. Finding a place to live, choosing a day-care centre or school, opening a bank account, using public transport and learning the driving code: all these aspects of life entail bureaucratic processes and local regulations that the managers find unfamiliar and often opaque.

- *A greatly extended acclimatization phase.* Managers making a leadership transition abroad often need considerably more time – up to twice as long – to start in their new functions than if they transfer within their own country. They have to invest time in understanding the new work environment and in building personal relationships. If used properly, however, this effort can prove to be an extraordinarily sound investment because it can help the manager establish international synergies and multicultural teams.

WHAT CAN YOU DO?

- Form as objective a picture as possible of the cultural and linguistic habits and rules of the game, especially in the preparation phase and first weeks of your new position. Focus not only on the situation at headquarters but also on the country and its people. Getting to know the culture of the country and of the specific region in which headquarters is located will facilitate interaction with your new colleagues. It will also help you gain insights into the corporate culture at headquarters.

- Learn the language of the host country. It is the only way for you to build business and private relationships effectively. Knowledge of the host language also facilitates your understanding of the cultural and social conventions and helps you rapidly integrate into the community.

- Clarify your specific assignment and analyse what both the subsidiary and headquarters expect of you.

- Identify potential misunderstandings arising out of cultural differences.

- Talk with seasoned managers from foreign subsidiaries about your experiences, and learn from their knowledge and insights. It is equally important to cultivate relations with local employees.

- Treat your assignment to corporate headquarters as a unique learning opportunity. It will enable you to improve your communication skills and your understanding of corporate business processes as well as to establish relationships and create important networks for your future career in the company. All of these assets will be very valuable when you return to operations in your own country.

Building blocks	The manager from a foreign subsidiary
1. Managing expectations	Prepare for the new culture by gathering information on conventions, the setting and the lifestyle in the country and specific region where headquarters is located.
2. Building key relationships	Build up a network and develop your key relationships. Be communicative.
3. Analysing the situation	Identify potential traps and cultural differences. Familiarize yourself with the organizational culture and processes at headquarters.
4. Establishing goals	Keep in mind what both your subsidiary and headquarters expect of management.
5. Fostering a climate for change	Show appreciation for your employees and foster open communication with them.
6. Initiating changes	Focus the assignment in order to initiate changes effectively. Keep in mind the special way things are done at headquarters.
7. Using symbols and rituals	Be sensitive to the typical rituals and linguistic and cultural barriers at headquarters.

Figure 59 Summary of Case Study 7

Further reading

Beer, M (1990) Why change programs don't produce change, *Harvard Business Review*, **6**

Gabarro, J J (1987) *The Dynamics of Taking Charge*, Harvard Business School Press, Boston

Gilmore, T N (1988) *Making a Leadership Change: How organizations and leaders can handle leadership transactions successfully*, Jossey-Bass, San Francisco

Jeannet, J-P (2000) *Managing with a Global Mindset*, Financial Times Management, London

Kotter, J P (1996) *Leading Change*, Harvard Business School Press, Boston

Kouzes, J M and Posner, B Z (2003) *The Leadership Challenge*, 3rd edn, Jossey-Bass, San Francisco

Moran, R T and Reisenberger, J R (1997) *The Global Challenge – Building the new worldwide enterprise*, McGraw-Hill, Maidenhead, Berkshire

Nadler, D A, Spencer J L and associates (1998) Executive Teams, Jossey-Bass, San Francisco

Peters, T J and Waterman, R H (2004) *In Search of Excellence: Lessons from America's best-run companies*, Collins, London

Pfeffer, J (1992) *Managing with Power: Politics and influence in organizations*, Harvard Business School Press, Boston

Index

NB: page numbers in *italic* indicate figures

The new *Creating Success* series

Published in association with **THE SUNDAY TIMES**

ISBN 10: 0 7494 4751 6
ISBN 13: 978 0 7494 4751 9
Paperback 2006

ISBN 10: 0 7494 4558 0
ISBN 13: 978 0 7494 4558 4
Paperback 2006

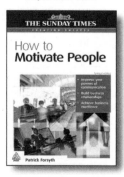

ISBN 10: 0 7494 4551 3
ISBN 13: 978 0 7494 4551 5
Paperback 2006

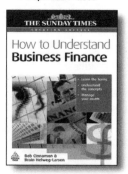

ISBN 10: 0 7494 4668 4
ISBN 13: 978 0 7494 4668 0
Paperback 2006

ISBN 10: 0 7494 4553 X
ISBN 13: 978 0 7494 4553 9
Paperback 2006

ISBN 10: 0 7494 4554 8
ISBN 13: 978 0 7494 4554 6
Paperback 2006

Order now at www.kogan-page.co.uk

KOGAN
PAGE

The new *Creating Success* series

Published in association with **THE SUNDAY TIMES**

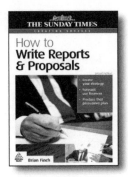

ISBN 10: 0 7494 4552 1
ISBN 13: 978 0 7494 4552 2
Paperback 2006

ISBN 10: 0 7494 4550 5
ISBN 13: 978 0 7494 4550 8
Paperback 2006

ISBN 10: 0 7494 4560 2
ISBN 13: 978 0 7494 4560 7
Paperback 2006

ISBN 10: 0 7494 4561 0
ISBN 13: 978 0 7494 4561 4
Paperback 2006

ISBN 10: 0 7494 4559 9
ISBN 13: 978 0 7494 4559 1
Paperback 2006

ISBN 10: 0 7494 4665 X
ISBN 13: 978 0 7494 4665 9
Paperback 2006

ALSO AVAILABLE FROM KOGAN PAGE

Sign up to receive regular e-mail updates on Kogan Page books at
www.kogan-page.co.uk/signup.aspx or:

Order now at www.kogan-page.co.uk

ALSO AVAILABLE FROM KOGAN PAGE

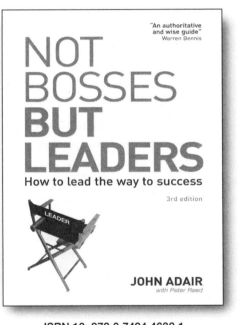

Sign up to receive regular e-mail updates on Kogan Page books at
www.kogan-page.co.uk/signup.aspx or:

Order now at www.kogan-page.co.uk

Fischer GroupInternational

The experts for successful Leadership Transitions

fgi Fischer Group International GmbH
Hudtwalckerstraße 11
D 22299 Hamburg
Germany

Phone +49-40-65 68 90 0
Fax   +49-40-65 68 90 80
info@fgi-mail.com
www.fgi-web.com

Fischer Group International
We are a management consulting firm with partners in the United States, Europe and Japan. For more than 15 years, fgi has been supporting executives with their leadership transitions and consulted in the areas of organizational change processes, strategy review and leadership development. In addition to a range of approaches, from executive coaching to global programmes and large-scale events, fgi offers one of the first interactive online tools for leadership transition support. Since 2004 a personalized online tool allows executives to track the different phases and activities of their Leadership Transitions and offers a wealth of information, hints and tips for how to get established in a new role. Go to www.fgi-lto.com to find out more about Leadership Transition Online.